Wild Life on the Rockies

LONG'S PEAK FROM THE EAST

Wild Life on the Rockies

By
Enos A. Mills

With Illustrations from Photographs

Introduction and Notes
by James H. Pickering

University of Nebraska Press
Lincoln and London

First Bison Book printing: 1988
Most recent printing indicated by the first digit below:
1   2   3   4   5   6   7   8   9   10

Library of Congress Cataloging-in-Publication Data
Mills, Enos Abijah, 1870–1922.
    Wild life on the Rockies.
    Reprint. Originally published: Boston: Houghton
Mifflin, 1909.
    "Bison book."
    Includes index.
    1. Mills, Enos Abijah, 1870–1922. 2. Pioneers—
Colarado—Biography. 3. Estes Park Region (Colo.)
4. Natural history—Colorado. 5. Colarado—Biography.
6. Longs Peak (Colo.) 7. Rocky Mountain National
Park (Colo.)—History. I. Pickering, James H.
II. Title.
F781.M45A3   1988   978.8′6903′0924   87-30203
ISBN 0-8032-3123-7
ISBN 0-8032-8152-8 (pbk.)

This Bison Book reproduces the 1909 edition published by Houghton
Mifflin Company. To this edition an introduction, a chronology, and notes
for the entire volume have been added.

To
John Muir

Contents

Illustrations

Illustrations

Introduction
By James H. Pickering

> Thousands of tired, nerve-shaken, over-civilized people are begin-
> ning to find out that going to the mountains is going home; that
> wilderness is a necessity; and that mountain parks and reservations
> are useful not only as fountains of timber and irrigating rivers, but
> as fountains of life.
>
> —John Muir, *Our National Parks* (1901)

For the first quarter of the twentieth century the names Enos Mills
and Estes Park were virtually synonymous. Mills's base of operations was his rustic mountain inn at the foot of Longs Peak, where
he wrote some sixteen books and scores of magazine and newspaper articles familiarizing the nation with the scenic wonders and
animal life of the Rocky Mountain West. When not writing or personally entertaining guests at Longs Peak Inn with fireside lectures or accompanying them on interpretive nature walks to
nearby beaver ponds, Mills was crisscrossing the country giving
public lectures, first on forestry and the need to protect the wilderness and later, after 1909, on behalf of his own special project,
the Rocky Mountain National Park.

Despite the apparent candor and simple directness of his books
and articles, Enos Abijah Mills (1870–1922) was a complex and
often contradictory man, the sort of man about whom stories, legends, and controversy easily gathered. Emerson Lynn, who came
to Longs Peak Inn as a driver in 1917 and was the Inn's manager
at the time of Mills's death five years later, offered a retrospective
view that is perhaps typical of those who were closest to Enos Mills:

> During the 15 years prior to his death in 1922, [Enos Mills was]
> the most colorful man in the Estes Park community. . . . He was re-

spected by many, ridiculed by others, hated by a few, and loved by
those who knew him best. Mills was a professed atheist who wor-
shiped nature. He was a Socialist who believed in the free enterprise system. He was a naturalist who cared nothing for natural
sciences. . . . He had a keen mind but simply ignored facts if they
conflicted with his pet causes. Here are a few of the legends about
him that I remember. 1) That he engaged in a gun fight over water
rights with Steve Hewes [a near neighbor] in which a man was killed.
2) That he charged for interviews and autographs. 3) That he did
not experience the incidents described in his books. 4) That he
promoted the Rocky Mountain National Park for personal gain. 5)
That he permitted no ministers or priests to stop at Long's Peak Inn.
6) That he ate no meat. 7) That Long's Peak Inn blew a curfew each
night at 10 and all lights had to be out 15 minutes later. To the best
of my knowledge each of these legends is false. I discussed several
of them with him from time to time. . . . Granted that he was eccentric and, at times, difficult to understand, I found Enos Mills to
be a loyal, sympathetic friend. He faithfully kept every promise and
was scrupulously honest.[1]

Lynn might also have mentioned that Enos Mills was a highly tem-
peramental man whose quarrels over the years involved not only
many of his closest neighbors but both the Forest Service and the
National Park Service, the two government agencies that seemed
best equipped to implement his own wilderness agenda. Most of
these battles, however, were waged behind the scenes and never
directly touched the public reputation that Mills created through
his books, articles, and public appearances. For many Americans,
Enos Mills remained to the end of his life the most accessible and
attractive writer-naturalist of his generation.

Enos Abijah Mills was the third youngest of the eleven children of
Enos A. Mills, Sr. (1834–1910) and his wife, Ann Lamb Mills (1837–
1923). Born and raised on the family farm, some five miles south
of the town of Pleasanton in Linn County, Kansas, Enos Mills's
childhood was marred by a digestive ailment that left him sickly
and weak, unable at times to attend school and clearly unsuited
for farm labor. When his condition had not improved by the age

of fourteen, he was encouraged by his mother and the family doctor to seek better health in the mountains of Colorado. Both parents and their cousin Elkanah J. Lamb had spent several months in 1860 searching for gold in the streams around Breckinridge. Ann Lamb, in fact, had "the distinction of being the first white woman that ever crossed the range west of Tarryall."[2] Though those few months yielded little gold, they did yield a lifetime of memories. "The first thing I remember in my life," Enos Mills later recalled, "was my mother telling me of her experiences in the high mountains of Colorado—during the summer of 1860. She told me of the green forests, the snow-fields, the clear, cold water, the high mountains, the wild flowers, all at hand right in summer."[3]

At the time of Enos Mills's first arrival during the summer of 1884, the sparsely settled valley of Estes Park differed but little from that day in mid-October 1859 when Joel Estes and one of his sons, following the Little Thompson River westward into the mountains on a exploring expedition, entered upon the scenic valley (or "park" in mountain parlance) that would soon bear their name. Change, however, was in the air, including the beginnings of a summer resort industry. Though hunting was no longer a major attraction, thanks to the hunting parties of the 1870s that had virtually wiped out the once teeming elk herds and greatly reduced the big horn sheep population, a growing number of summer visitors found Estes Park to be a safe, scenic, healthful, and increasingly accessible place to vacation. They came to fish, ride, and climb mountains, or simply to recreate among spectacular and invigorating mountain scenery that Colorado boosters insisted was fully equal to the Alps of Switzerland. Visitors in 1884 had their choice of accommodations. They could stay at the fancy and comparatively expensive fifty-room English Hotel erected in 1877 by Windham Thomas Wyndham-Quinn, the fourth Earl of Dunraven,[4] or at one of the less pretentious guest "ranches" operated for summer tourists by such early Estes Park pioneers as Elkanah Lamb, Abner Sprague, William James, Alexander MacGregor, and Horace Ferguson.[5] Many preferred simply to camp along the banks of the Big Thompson or Fall rivers, or by one of their tributary streams.

Though Enos Mills himself apparently never acknowledged the

fact, his choice of destination was by no means accidental. For almost a decade, Estes Park had been the home of his father's cousin, the Reverend Elkanah Lamb (1832–1915), a minister of the Church of the United Brethren. In 1875 Parson Lamb had built in Longs Peak Valley, some nine miles south of and fifteen hundred feet above the site of the future village, the twelve-by-fourteen-foot cabin that would evolve into Longs Peak House, the forerunner of Enos Mills's famous Longs Peak Inn.[6] Shortly thereafter, Lamb was augmenting his preacher's salary by raising cattle, putting up tourists, and guiding parties to the summit of Longs Peak for five dollars a trip. "If they would not pay for spiritual guidance," he wrote in his memoirs, "I compelled them to divide for material elevation."[7] From a parental point of view, there could have been few better people to enlist in watching over the career of a sickly but determined boy of fourteen.

Mills spent the summer of 1884 doing chores and odd jobs at William James's Elkhorn Lodge and then returned to the plains of eastern Colorado, where he spent the winter of 1884–85 working on a cattle ranch. By spring he was back in Estes Park, this time working for Elkanah Lamb and his son Carlyle. Though the buildings that formed Lamb's Longs Peak House were modest, their setting was spectacular. Set in the heavily wooded natural amphitheater known as Longs Peak Valley, the Lamb homestead was bounded on the west by the towering precipice of 14,256-foot Longs Peak and its two guardian neighbors, Mount Meeker and Mount Lady Washington, and on the east by the craggy peaks of the mountain called the Twin Sisters. It was here in this sequestered and still largely unexplored upland valley, with its gentle slopes of spruce and lodgepole pines intermixed with stands of willow and aspen, its active beaver ponds, and its meadows of wild flowers, that Enos Mills would build his own homestead cabin in 1885–86. Long before he took over the guest ranch of the Lambs in 1902, this valley served as Enos Mills's inspiration, as well as his place of refuge and retreat. It was his relationship to this special place that he tried to share with the world. "He who in Estes Park spends time by peak and stream," he wrote in one of his earliest published essays,

breathing the rosiny air, drinking the pure water—holding com-
munion with Nature—seeing the bright sun and the blue sky, lin-
gering over scenes and sunsets, listening, in shadowy forests, to the
melodious tone of the wood thrush; or who feels a strange longing
when the lonely moon gives light, mystery and shadow, or sleeps
under the wide and starry sky—he who thus, for a time, enriches
existence, will go away from its pictures to hate less, with existence
extended—and life sweetened and intensified.[8]

Here in Longs Peak Valley and on its adjacent mountain heights
Mills gained much of the first-hand knowledge of the wilderness
that would inform his career. It was also from this spot, beginning
in 1885, that he set out in every season and at every hour to climb
to the top of Longs Peak, a destination which he achieved forty
times alone and two hundred and fifty-seven times in acting as a
guide for others.

For Enos Mills, as for countless other health seekers, the climate
of the mountains acted as a restorative. By the age of seventeen
he was strong enough to make his way to the copper mines of
Butte, Montana, to take up a career that would occupy most of his
winters for the next fifteen years. The Anaconda Mine, where he
began working as a tool boy and where he rose through a series
of jobs to the position of engineer, offered good wages and a work
schedule that allowed him to leave for long periods of time to explore the out-of-doors. As an added benefit, Butte offered a first-
rate public library, from which Mills borrowed extensively.

Enos Mills's life-long belief in self-improvement began with his
own education. The frontier world of Colorado and Montana in
which he landed tended to reward men of action, and most young
men in Mills's circumstances would no doubt have been content
to get by with whatever rudiments of formal education they
brought with them. Not so with Enos Mills. Though he "escaped
most of public school and missed college,"[9] Mills inherited from
his mother "a love of good books" and the determination and self-
discipline to learn on his own. His reading, however eclectic, was
well directed—Shakespeare, Cervantes, Dickens, Thackeray, By-
ron, Stevenson, Scott, Emerson, Irving, and Whitman; the nature
writings of Thoreau, Burroughs, and (after 1894) John Muir;

books of travel and history; and the works of such progressive thinkers as Darwin, Huxley, Tyndall, Spencer, and Ingersoll. Books, in fact, became one of Enos Mills's most treasured possessions. "I bought quite a number of books this fall," he notes in one early letter, "and Elkanah [Lamb] favored me with a substantial bookcase."[10] In later years more than one visitor to Longs Peak Inn would remark on the hundreds of books lining the walls of the three-room cabin that housed his private study.

To improve his writing skills and penmanship, Mills adopted at an early age the classic method of keeping a commonplace book into which he copied bits and pieces of information for later use. He also used its pages as a place to write out practice essays, initially on general topics like "American Liberty," but increasingly on subjects growing out of his own wilderness experience. His writing skills improved greatly over the years, and though Enos Mills would never be the literary equal of a John Muir or John Burroughs, he did develop a style and set of techniques that were well adapted to his subject matter and to the audience he sought to entertain and educate.

Winters in Butte purchased summers of freedom, and Mills used them well. Beginning with the still largely unexplored region adjacent to Longs Peak, Mills set out to learn the mountains. Clad in a worn sack suit that became a kind of uniform and hatless save in the most inclement weather, Mills dispensed with tent, bedroll, and cooking utensils in favor of an outfit consisting of matches, candle, small folding ax, tin cup, sweater, Kodak camera, and a small notebook in which to record his observations. For food he carried with him pocketfuls of raisins, sometimes mixed with chocolate, which he insisted could satisfy his nutritional needs in any season. He also made a conscious decision early on not to carry a gun, without which all objects were so changed that he had only a "dim recollection of having seen the place before" (see pp. 77–78). Gradually over the years his sphere of wilderness exploring and adventuring widened, to the point that Mills was finally able to boast that "in Alaska, Canada, Mexico, and in every state in the Union I have sat by a camp-fire alone."[11] It was a solitary sort of existence that Mills sought, but where others might have experienced loneliness, Mills seems to have felt only the exhilaration of one who is truly at peace with himself and at home in the world.

It was on one of these early excursions away from the mines, in December 1889, that Mills had an accidental meeting with John Muir (1838–1914), who had already gained considerable attention for his efforts to preserve the Yosemite Valley from the incursions of civilization. "On the beach near the old cliff house [in San Francisco's Golden Gate Park]," Mills later recalled, "I came upon a number of people around a small gray bearded little man who had a hand full of plants which he was explaining. . . . As soon as the people scattered I asked him concerning a long-rooted plant that someone had dug from a sand dune."[12] Muir answered the young man's questions: "Then he invited me for a four mile walk across the sand hills and through Golden Gate Park to the end of the car line." He also apparently challenged Mills on the subject of vocation. This chance encounter with Muir became the turning point of Enos Mills's life. Muir's questions and observations transformed his somewhat aimless appreciation of nature and love of the outdoors into a passionate commitment on behalf of wilderness preservation. "You have helped me more than all others," he told Muir in January 1913 in the midst of the campaign for Rocky Mountain National Park; "but for you I might never have done anything for scenery."[13] "I owe everything to Muir," he wrote in 1917. "If it hadn't been for him I would have been a mere gypsy."[14] Muir became Mills's lifelong inspiration and role model: what "John of the Mountains" had been to Yosemite and the Sierras of California, Enos Mills would become for the Colorado Rockies.

Mills's meeting with Muir gave direction to the decade that followed. It was a decade of travel—to California, Nevada, Wyoming, Alaska, and the Midwest—and of new initiatives. In the fall of 1895, Mills gave his first speech on forestry in Kansas City and about the same time he began writing articles about Estes Park and the scenery of Colorado, often illustrated with his own photographs, for the Sunday supplement of the *Denver Republican*. In 1896, and for a number of summers thereafter, Mills collected news items for the Denver papers by riding on horseback among the widely scattered ranches and resorts of Estes Park, for which he was paid one-third cent per word. Mills also used the occasion to gather up the stories about the park's pioneer settlers and other bits and pieces of local history that would go into the making of his first published book, *The Story of Estes Park and a Guide Book* (1905).

The winter of 1901–2 was Mills's last in Butte. The following summer he fulfilled a lifelong dream by buying Longs Peak House from Carlyle Lamb.[15] Thanks to its strategic location at the foot of Longs Peak—some three thousand feet below its spectacular East Face—the Lambs' ranch had long since established a reputation as a base for mountaineers setting out for the summit, some eight miles distant. It was from the ranch that the intrepid Isabella Bird, accompanied by the legendary "Rocky Mountain Jim" Nugent, set forth on her famous October 1873 conquest of Longs Peak, later described so graphically in *A Lady's Life in the Rocky Mountains* (1879). It was also from here, some fourteen years later, that Connecticut druggist Frederick H. Chapin, accompanied by Carlyle Lamb, made the climb to the summit that became the focus of his classic *Mountaineering in Colorado: The Peaks about Estes Park*, published by the Appalachian Mountain Club in 1889 and reprinted by the University of Nebraska Press in 1987.

Under Mills's supervision Longs Peak House—which he renamed Longs Peak Inn in 1904—was enlarged and expanded. Though the main lodge, including a recently enlarged dining room, burned to the ground in June 1906, the setback proved to be only temporary. The Longs Peak Inn that Mills reopened for business on July 4th of the same year would become one of most distinctive and best known summer hostelries in the nation.

For the rebuilding of the low, two-story main building, which together with ten cabins comprised Longs Peak Inn, Mills selected a mixture of fire-killed and wind-carved trees, whose unusual natural features gave the new inn a unique appearance. Visitors caught the spirit of the place immediately:

> The setting is most inspiring. The collection of buildings occupy the center of a wide amphitheater in a glacial meadow as green and flower-strewn as any peaceful valley at sea level. Peaks arise in magnificent terraces, their base covered thickly with aspens and spruce and pine, their sides garmented in dark pine foliage. . . .[16]

The reception room strikes one as being unusually unique and attractive with its trimmings of weathered pines, beaver cut logs, and old-fashioned fire-place with its iron tea kettles. The tables, the bases of which are the roots of old trees, and a screen in front of the dining-room door, a cross section of an immense root, being about 16-feet square, and forming a most beautiful lattice work, is very odd in appearance. The only finished wood one senses is the door and window casings.[17]

What a secluded, quaint place it is. The inn is built entirely of pine logs and in its furnishings the native timber is everywhere in evidence. The quaint old porch stands directly over a murmuring stream. The owner of the place is Mr. Enos A. Mills, the author of *Wild Life in [sic] the Rockies*. He has a unique personality; he is a law unto himself, wears a hat only when he pleases and under no circumstances will he don evening dress. Nowhere could a man be found more in keeping with his surroundings.[18]

At the height of the season Longs Peak Inn entertained upwards of a hundred guests and employed a staff of thirty-five, made up mostly of college students and schoolteachers. The Inn was run as a "non-tip house" whose rules were well established and absolute: there was to be no drinking, dancing, music, or card playing. Apparently, it was not so much that these diversions offended Mills's moral sense but rather that, with so much nature to attend to, such forms of city entertainment were simply irrelevant. Firearms and pets—with the single exception of Mills's faithful collie Scotch—were similarly prohibited. Those who disregarded Mills's rules were summarily treated; and more than one offender, rumor had it, found himself excluded from the premises, his reservations canceled. Mills personally supervised every aspect of the operation—including the amount of coffee used in the urns. And though he made it a practice not to dine with his guests, the presence of the energetic Mills, with his ruddy face, broad forehead, and shock of carrot-colored hair, was everywhere in evidence. Following the dinner meal Mills frequently delivered impromptu nature talks from the bottom step of the split-log stairway in the Inn's main room, after which he would bid his guests good-night and then retire to the quiet privacy of his own cabin for an evening of reading and writing. Needing little sleep himself, Mills was up and about early, challenging his guests with the cheerful greeting: "Glad you're living?"

Longs Peak Inn, above all, became the extension of its owner-proprietor. Under Mills's direction the Inn had what his manager, Emerson Lynn, described as a "unique and piquant flavor. He [Mills] kept it rather austere but bouncing with life, sparkling conversation, a controversial but kindly atmosphere and an indescribable patina of opulence melded with severe simplicity."[19] Over the years thousands of summer visitors (including Otis Skinner, Edna Ferber, William Allen White, Gene Stratton Porter, Clarence Darrow, Charles Evans Hughes, Douglas Fairbanks, Sr., Jane Addams, and Horace Lorimer, the influential editor of the *Saturday Evening Post* and an active force in the national parks movement) sought out the hospitality and the education that Mills worked hard to provide. An inscription on the doorpost in the form of a sixteen-line poem addressed "To Whom It May Concern!" succinctly announced to arriving guests the kind of deportment expected: "What will you with our bodies,/ Rude ravisher of flowers./ Despoiler of our loveliness/ To please your idle hours?"[20] Those who insisted on continuing to play the role of tourist were not infrequently treated to a strong dose of acerbic wit. "I hear there is some fine scenery up here," one new arrival is supposed to have said. "Where do I go to see it?" To which Mills dryly responded, "You must have been misinformed."[21]

The year 1902 was also marked by Enos Mills's first major publication, an article entitled "A Western Artist" that was published in *Outdoor Life.* Drawing his subject matter from his own store of wilderness adventures, Enos Mills thus launched a career as a popular author that would in little more than a decade propel him into the front ranks of America's growing conservation movement. For someone whose life was often preoccupied with other things, including the not inconsiderable task of running a large mountain inn, Enos Mills proved to be a remarkably prolific author. The medium he chose—both big-circulation magazines like the *Saturday Evening Post, Atlantic, World's Work, Colliers,* and *Harper's,* and more specialized country, outdoor, and juvenile magazines like *Craftsman, Country Gentlemen, Sunset, Country Life, American Boy,* and *Youth's Companion*—was particularly well suited not only to his personal inclinations and writing habits but to his goal of bringing his message to a large and diverse national audience. Magazines, moreover, paid ready cash, a not inconsiderable benefit for someone whose major source of income was decidedly seasonal. With the exception of the brief anecdotal history of Estes Park that he published at his own expense in 1905, Mills did not, however, attempt a book-length volume until 1909. In that year he persuaded the well-known Boston firm of Houghton Mifflin, which already counted John Muir and John Burroughs among its stable of established nature writers, to bring out the miscellany entitled *Wild Life on the Rockies*. With its publication, Enos Mills achieved the status of a major author.

The period between 1902 and 1915 brought virtually uninterrupted success; in many respects it marked the zenith of Mills's career. It began with a curious, though highly romantic, interlude during the winters of 1903 to 1906, when, at the invitation of the State Irrigation Department and its head L. G. Carpenter, Mills served as Colorado's official State Snow Observer. In this capacity it was Mills's assignment to "traverse the upper slopes of the Rockies"—one winter he followed the Continental Divide from the Wyoming line south to New Mexico—measuring the snow accumulation at the headwaters of streams in order to anticipate the spring and summer runoff. Mills's colorful mountaintop adventuring did not go unnoticed. Coupled with the increasing exposure he received as a published magazine and newspaper writer and as a public lecturer, such activities greatly boosted Enos Mills's reputation and authority. They also brought him to the attention of President Theodore Roosevelt, who in January 1907 invited him to serve as special "Government Lecturer on Forestry" under Gifford Pinchot, the aggressive head of Roosevelt's new Forest Service.

Conservation occupied a high place on the list of Roosevelt's priorities for the nation. T. R. himself, of course, had long been an advocate of the "strenuous life" and the virtues of wilderness living, and by the time he assumed the presidency in 1901 the country was ready to respond to a program that made the conservation of natural resources into official government policy. Part of that policy dictated an expanded role for the Bureau of Forestry, which in 1905 had been transferred from the Department of the Interior to the Department of Agriculture, together with the 85.6 million acres of forest reserves for which it was responsible, and renamed the Forest Service. Two years later these reserves—now totaling some 150 million acres—were renamed National Forests. Pinchot, Roosevelt's most trusted adviser on matters dealing with conservation, was a master of public relations and very much aware of the need to court public opinion at a time when he was seeking to consolidate and expand the power of his new agency. ("Use the press first, last, and all the time," he told his subordinates in 1907, "if you want to reach the public.")[22] The appointment of someone of Mills's emerging stature clearly made sense, particularly since much of the opposition to the Roosevelt-Pinchot program came from the West, where the largest national forests were located; from citizens who tended to view any restrictions on timber, grazing, mining, and water rights as a plot by the eastern establishment to wrest away local control and stifle economic growth. What better way to sell their new forestry program than by employing a westerner to deliver the message?

Mills served as an independent lecturer on forestry from January 1907 to May 1909 at a salary of $2,400 per year plus expenses. Roosevelt's appointment thrust Enos Mills into the national arena and gave him a platform on which to present the case for forest conservation and to promote his growing preoccupation with the recreational and aesthetic uses of the wilderness. Mills made the most of the opportunity. His surviving itinerary for one seven-month period (October 1908 to May 1909) lists some hundred and forty lecture engagements in thirty-six states before high school and college groups, teachers' organizations, women's and men's clubs, various kinds of civic and business gatherings, before anyone, in short, who stood ready to listen to his message (a message more often than not entitled "Our Friends the Trees"). The reviews were almost uniformly excellent. "The lecture," a Helena, Montana, reporter told his readers in 1907, " was an odd but effective mixture of sentiment and sense: an illumination of both the practicality and poetry of forestry."[23] Others found Mills witty and entertaining, brown sack suit and all: "a performer of consummate skill, able, singlehandedly, to enchant a crowd for an entire evening."[24]

Such a schedule, however repetitious and taxing, produced rich dividends in terms of public exposure and widened national reputation. Together with his publications, these lectures helped to create a public image that, whatever his other troubles, would stand Enos Mills in good stead for the remainder of his life. Americans came to see in Mills, as Carl Abbott has observed,

> a self-taught scientist with a firsthand understanding of the ecology of the high country, and as a man who reported his own experiences with grizzlies and and his own observations of pines and aspen. The Mills described in his essays [and the Mills who appeared on the lecture platform] was also a hero of timberline adventures, a man who had faced alone the perils of avalanche, storm, bitter cold, fierce winds, and snowblindness. The character he helped to fashion was strong and sympathetic.[25]

The six-year task to which Enos Mills turned his attention in 1909, culminating in the bill creating Rocky Mountain National Park that Woodrow Wilson signed into law on January 26, 1915, proved to be, in his own words, "the most strenuous and growth-compelling occupation I have ever followed."[26] To a large extent that campaign was the story of the promotional and lobbying efforts of one man: Enos Mills of Estes Park. To be sure, Mills had a good deal of help both regionally and nationally, especially from J. Horace McFarland's powerful American Civic Association, James Grafton Rogers and the Colorado Mountain Club, the Denver Chamber of Commerce, and from a broad coalition of civic and business organizations and state political leaders. Nevertheless, without Enos Mills's dogged persistence and determination it is conceivable that the "Estes Park Project," as Mills called it, might well have languished and died.

The formal proposal calling for the creation of a new national park in the Estes Park region apparently grew out of the suggestion made by H. N. Wheeler, head of the Medicine Bow National Forest, at an October 1907 meeting of the Estes Park Protection

and Improvement Association.[27] "I told them," Wheeler later recalled, "that one of the biggest assets of any recreation area is the
game, and if they wished to increase the value of their playground
they should create a game refuge."[28] Though Mills did not attend
this meeting, he did write Wheeler the following spring to ask just
where the boundaries of such a preserve might be located. It was
in the context of this exchange that Mills's own far more ambitious plan for a full-blown national park began to take shape.
Within days of the September 4, 1909, annual meeting of the Association, at which the village's civic and business leaders voted
unanimously to seek the help of the federal government in establishing the "Estes National Park and Game Preserve," Mills issued
for publication a proposal of his own:

> Around Estes Park, Colorado, are mountain scenes of excep-
> tional beauty and grandeur. In this territory is Longs Peak and one
> of the most rugged sections of the Continental Divide of the Rock-
> ies. The region is almost entirely above the altitude of 7,500 feet,
> and in it are forests, streams, waterfalls, snowy peaks, great canons,
> glaciers, scores of species of wild birds, and more than a thousand
> varieties of wild flowers.
>
> In many respects this section is losing its wild charms. Extensive
> areas of primeval forests have been misused and ruined; saw-mills
> are humming and cattle are in the wild gardens! The once numer-
> ous big game has been hunted out of existence and the picturesque
> beaver are almost gone.
>
> These scenes are already extensively used as places of recrea-
> tion. If they are to be permanently and more extensively used and
> preserved it will be necessary to hold them as public property and
> protect them within a national park.[29]

The third and final paragraph of this proclamation suggests how
far Mills and his fellow conservationists had come in their thinking about wilderness preservation. Though the Forest Service,
under both Pinchot and Henry Graves, who succeeded him as chief
forester in February 1910, professed their interest in national
parks and scenic preservation, their main commitment was to a
policy of "preservation through use" that made the nation's forest
preserves available to lumbering and grazing interests, albeit un-

der controlled, "scientific," conditions. Such a policy did not totally reject the recreational and aesthetic uses of the wilderness, but it did mean, as Muir discovered in the fight over building a reservoir for the city of San Francisco in Yosemite's Hetch Hetchy Valley, that in conflicts between wise-use conservationists and strict preservationists the utilitarian forces would inevitably emerge victorious.[30] Given the Forest Service's clear biases (biases of which John Muir and most other scenic preservationists had been long aware) Mills's two-year assignment as lecturer becomes somewhat difficult to understand. Once enlightened, however, Mills's reaction was extreme and uncompromising. The hatred of the Forest Service that he developed during the course of his six-year campaign for Rocky Mountain National Park was so strong, in fact, that it eventually embarrassed and even alienated staunch supporters like McFarland and Rogers.[31]

During the two years following the distribution of Mills's September 1909 proclamation, the Wheeler-Mills proposal slowly gathered support. It gained major new impetus in January 1913 with the release of an enthusiastically positive recommendation from Robert B. Marshall of the U. S. Geological Survey, who had been dispatched to the Estes Park area the previous fall to study the feasibility of a national park.[32] Within weeks of Marshall's report the first park bill, drafted by Rogers, was introduced in Congress and the battle for Rocky Mountain National Park was at last fully joined. Victory did not come easily, or at least not as easily as Mills and others had hoped. Opposition arose from the expected quarters: from cattlemen jealous of their grazing prerogatives, from mining and timber interests, from farmers along Colorado's eastern slopes who were concerned about continuing access to their watersheds. There was also the Forest Service, which, at the very least, was guilty of footdragging. All of these groups had to be won over, neutralized, or otherwise contended with. There was also the intricacy and built-in lethargy of the legislative process itself. In the end it took three separate park bills, five major revisions, and almost two years to move the desired legislation through Congress, by which time Marshall's 700 square miles had been reduced to 358.5, far short of Enos Mills's original proposal that had called for 1,000.[33]

The energetic Enos Mills was active on every front, using his in-

creased accessibility to local and national newspapers and magazines, as well as the lecture platform on which he is said to have
made more than three hundred appearances,[34] to carry the campaign for Rocky Mountain National Park to the public. His message was a simple but effective one: contact with the wilderness
encourages physical and mental vigor and the building of character. To the extent that national parks keep American tourists at
home, they stimulate the economy and promote national unity. A
five-month lecture trip during the winter and early spring of 1911–
12 took him eastward through Kansas City, Omaha, St. Louis,
Chicago, and Indianapolis to Washington and a December appearance at the annual meeting of McFarland's American Civic
Association. When not lecturing or giving interviews, Mills was
holding private meetings with potential allies to drum up support
for his new park. In late December 1914, Mills appeared before
the hearing on the park bill conducted by the House Committee
on the Public Lands, where he was introduced by Colorado Rep-
resentative Edward T. Taylor as "one of the noted naturalists,
travelers, authors, and lecturers of this country, who has made a
great study of this question [the park bill] and has lived in the park
for a great many years, and knows almost every foot of it, and is
probably better qualified to speak on the park than anyone else."[35]
Both before and after the hearing, Mills was on the road lobbying
on behalf of national parks and "kindred subjects"—in Omaha,
Chicago, Peoria, St. Louis, Indianapolis, Columbus, and elsewhere. Even the peripatetic Mills, who finally reached home on
snowshoes in late February, found the pace to be one that "anni-
hilates me."[36]

Following the final passage of park bill on January 18, 1915,
Enos Mills received his due in the form of tribute and commend-
ation. The *Denver Post*, in announcing the victory in its January
20th edition, carried on the front page a congratulatory cartoon
of a smiling Colorado shaking hands with Mills and saying "Enos,
I'm Proud of You!" Nine months later, on September 4, 1915, upon
the occasion of the formal dedication of the new park, the *Post* once
again publicly thanked Mills and bestowed upon him the title of
"Father of Rocky Mountain National Park." The ceremonies of
that day in Horseshoe Park undoubtedly marked the culmination

of Enos Mills's public career. Though dignitaries such as Colorado Governor George Carlson, Congressman Edward Taylor, and Assistant Secretary of the Interior Stephen T. Mather were numbered among the some three hundred assembled guests, the day emphatically belonged to Enos Mills, who, appropriately, served as master of ceremonies. His own remarks were both eloquent and prophetic: "In years to come when I am asleep forever beneath the pines, thousands of families will find rest and hope in this park, and on through the years others will come and be happy in the splendid scenes that I helped to save for them."[37]

Unfortunately, such equanimity and sense of accomplishment did not last. Though Mills was now free to return to the life he enjoyed most as writer-naturalist and proprietor of Longs Peak Inn, it was not long before his sense of indignation was once again aroused against a government agency. This time the object of Mills's antagonism was the National Park Service, whose very existence Mills, Muir, McFarland and other strict preservationists had come to believe was absolutely essential if the country's emerging park system was to be administered in a way that emphasized the aesthetic and recreational uses of the wilderness.[38]

Created by law in August 1916 as an agency within the Department of the Interior, over the heated objections of the Forest Service, the Park Service and its able first director, Stephen T. Mather, inspired great hope among preservationists. Moreover, Secretary of the Interior Franklin K. Lane's mandate was unmistakably clear: the Park Service must see to it that parks are "set apart for the use, observation, health, and pleasure of the people" and "maintained in absolutely unimpaired form for the use of future generations as well as those in our own time."[39] To implement such goals, Mather's first task, particularly with an eye to the annual appropriations process, was to build as broad as possible a network of support. Where the Forest Service could court, at least to some extent, agriculture, timber, mining, and power interests, these powerful constituencies had been deliberately excluded or curtailed by the Park Service's enabling legislation. Enemies of the new park system inevitably called attention to such restrictions on capitalistic free enterprise. Mather shrewdly reversed the equation. Linking the protection of scenery directly to economic growth and development, he sought the support of local and regional tourist interests with the realization that "those whose livelihoods came to depend on the existence of the parks could be counted on to defend them."[40] The establishment of concessions and a concessions policy thus received early attention. And it was precisely over this issue—the issue of the transportation concessions in Rocky Mountain National Park—that Enos Mills and Mather's new agency collided head-on and soon parted company.

The controversy over the decision made by Park Superintendent L. C. Way in the spring of 1919 to grant an exclusive franchise agreement for the Park to Roe Emery's Rocky Mountain Park Transportation Company was perhaps inevitable. In 1916, the year of its dedication, some 51,000 visitors entered the Park. In 1917, the number had more than doubled and by 1919 the total reached nearly 170,000, placing an intolerable burden on the park's limited system of roads. Clearly, something had to be done. The franchise agreement with Emery, who had successfully pioneered bus motor transportation in Glacier National Park and whose company had been operating in Rocky Mountain National Park since 1916, seemed to offer a reasonable solution to a growing problem.

Way's agreement with Emery, which was awarded without public discussion or competitive bids, effectively banned from the park independent rent-car (or "jitney") drivers who made their summer livings by transporting visitors to and from hotels or taking them on sightseeing excursions. Such entrepreneurs not only helped to keep the roads congested but, it was widely charged, frequently inflicted poor service and high prices upon their customers. One of the touring car services directly affected by the new ban originated at Enos Mills's Longs Peak Inn. Though most of Estes Park's hotel men seemed satisfied with the arrangement, Mills was not. Always sensitive to any affront, real or imaginary, Enos Mills saw the concessions agreement with Emery as an "illegal, unnecessary and unjust" monopoly established by arrogant bureaucrats indifferent to the public's right of free access to the nation's parks.[41] Mills had long-since condemned the Forest Service as "a big organization with almost irresponsible power" that "makes its own rulings; acts as judge and jury when those rulings are disputed."[42] By 1919 he had considerably broadened the indictment. "In the very nature of things," he told McFarland, "Bureaus, if they have any powers at all, are inevitably mostly bad."[43] Way's explanations and overtures were rebuffed. Instead, Mills determined to force a test case over the Park Service's legal right to establish such a concessions policy. On August 14, 1919, openly and with advanced warning, Mills dispatched a car from Longs Peak Inn into the park where it was intercepted by Way himself. Though the record indicates that Way made subsequent efforts to mollify and to compromise the issue, it was to no avail. "Mr. Mills," Way wrote his superiors on August 28, "is obsessed with the idea of fighting the concession policy in National Parks. He states that he now sees that the policy is wrong, and that in a short time the corporation that we are protecting will dominate the Park Service."[44]

Enos Mills sued Way in the U. S. District Court of Colorado for interfering with "his common rights as a citizen of the State of Colorado in traveling over the Park roads." Despite two rounds of court decisions that upheld the Park Service's right to regulate and denied Mills's claims, the issue smoldered without final resolution. Gradually it became part of a much larger legal issue involving a suit by the State of Colorado challenging the right of the federal government to regulate traffic over roads never formally ceded to the jurisdiction of the United States. This so-called "Cede Jurisdiction" controversy dragged on long past Enos Mills's death in September 1922.[45]

Fortunately for Enos Mills, whatever controversy marred these years, there were other sources of satisfaction. One was his writing career, which between 1916 and 1922 saw the publication of seven books. There were also lecture invitations to respond to, and the business of running Longs Peak Inn, whose facilities he enlarged in 1916 by doubling the size of the lobby and dining room to take advantage of the increasing number of summer visitors who came to Estes Park and its new national park.[46] In all three of these activities—writing, lecturing, and innkeeping—people saw Enos Mills at his best, most relaxed and warmest, and they responded accordingly. In each of these activities, as in his earlier adventuring alone among the mountains, Mills could meet and engage life on his own terms and according to his own rules. When he could not control the terms of the engagement, as for example in his skirmishes with both the Forest Service and the Park Service, Enos Mills often found himself in trouble.

In 1916 Enos Mills met Esther Burnell (1889–1946), a young woman of twenty-seven who like Enos himself had come to Estes Park in search of better health and stayed on to homestead. She also became his secretary and protégé and, on August 12, 1918, in a civil ceremony that took place in Mills's homestead cabin, his wife.[47] A year later, on April 27, 1919, their only child, a daughter named Enda, was born.

Though Enos Mills's life had taken a new turn, there was still the battle against the Park Service to fight. His weapon, as usual, was the written and spoken word. He published attacks on the transportation monopoly in the *New York Times* and *New Republic*. He traveled east seeking a hearing for his own personal vision of national parks—to Chicago, Pittsburgh, Cleveland, Columbus, New York, Springfield, and Boston. Though Mills was treated with politeness everywhere, his views, for the first time, apparently fell short of sparking the desired response. Still, Mills continued his new crusade.[48] In October 1921 he made a two-week tour of Texas to give his views on desirable sites for state parks. The next month he was in Los Angeles and San Diego. In early 1922, Mills again returned east. He got as far as New York, where, on his way to keep an engagement, he was involved in a bizarre subway collision in which he broke two ribs and punctured a lung.

Returning home, Mills almost immediately contracted the flu. Normally, he would have recovered quickly, even in winter, but this time Enos Mills was tired and worn out. Neighbors such as Charles Edwin Hewes noted the change.[49] So did Hewes's housekeeper Julia Morrissey, who observed Mills near the Inn in late March: "Instead of running briskly to and fro as he did formerly, and without hat or overcoat even in the coldest weather . . . he walks very slowly and wears a hat and overcoat closely buttoned up to his ears."[50] The coming of spring found him still exhausted: "I have been so miserable," he wrote to a friend, "that I have not written to you and as I am far from my best I shall not write you at length today."[51] Still things did not improve. Referring to Dean Babcock, another of Mills's near neighbors, Hewes noted in his August 2, 1922, journal entry, "Dean says that Enos Mills has lung trouble, pulmonary tuberculosis, was stricken in Washington, D.C. and came back a very sick man."[52] Though he apparently did not have tuberculosis, Babcock was correct: Enos Mills, who prided himself on his "extraordinary endurance," was very sick. Summer did not fully revive him, and, compounding his problems, in early September Mills suffered a severe abscess that required the removal of a portion of his jaw and several of his teeth. On the evening of September 21, 1922, Mills retired at the usual time, only to awaken his wife at 2:30 a.m. and tell her he was feeling very ill. A doctor from Chicago staying at the Inn was summoned, but within minutes, at 3:00 a.m. on the morning of September 22, 1922, Enos Mills was dead.[53]

Mills's own funeral directions, found in a letter in his desk, were simple: he was to be buried near his homestead cabin following a service at the Inn; there was to be no music, no prayers, no passages from the Bible.[54] The service, attended by some three hundred people, was conducted in the main lobby of Longs Peak Inn by Judge Ben Lindsey of Denver, a life-long friend. Lindsey spoke briefly and read three of Enos Mills's favorite poems—one by John Muir, one by John Burroughs, and one by Alfred Tennyson. At the conclusion, a party of twelve, consisting only of pallbearers and the immediate family, crossed the road to Mills's small cabin. The rest of the mourners stood outside the Inn, watching the burial from a distance. The onlookers were rewarded with a fitting *nunc dimittis*. Accounts agree that "as if by miracle, just as the casket began its slow descent into the rocks, the pall of grim, darkening storm towering across the face of Long's Peak was torn aside, and the red gold rays of the setting sun poured brilliantly thru the giant 'notch' upon the mountain's summit."[55]

Though Mills referred to his role in the establishment of Rocky Mountain National Park as "the achievement of my life," his legacy most certainly includes the sixteen books and countless articles that he wrote over a period of more than two decades. That Mills's writings are now for the most part out of print and forgotten is unfortunate, for in their day they not only enjoyed great popularity but helped to shape the attitude of a whole generation of Americans toward the wilderness. Mills made no secret of his purposes. "My chief aim in life," he wrote, "has been to arouse interest in the out of doors."[56] It was to this end that all of Mills's activities, including his writings, were directed.

Wild Life on the Rockies (1909), his first major book-length publication, is typical in both subject matter and approach. Though his perspective and style would mature over the years,[57] Mills discovered early in his career that his talents as writer lay in his ability to use incidents drawn from his own personal experience to tell a good story in a dramatic way. It was his ability as a storyteller coupled with the easy readability of his prose that appealed most strongly to his middle-class audience and accounted for much of his contemporary popularity. The straightforward stories Mills told of his wilderness adventures with snowslides, wild beasts, and even wilder weather were interesting, exciting, and fun—good reading on a quiet afternoon. They were also accessible to the average reader in a way that the more discursive and transcendental writings of a John Muir or a John Burroughs were not.

There were other reasons for Mills's popularity as well. Not the least of these, as one reviewer of *Wild Life on the Rockies* noted, was the charm of "the author's personality,"[58]—the intrinsically attractive character of the narrator that Mills establishes in the mind of his reader. "I had many experiences,—amusing, dangerous, and exciting," he announces in the first pages of his opening chapter. "There was abundance of life and fun in the work. On many an evening darkness captured me and compelled me to spend the night in the wilds without bedding, and often without food. During these nights I kept a camp-fire blazing until daylight released me" (p. 5).

This narrator, who is never far removed from the reader's view, is of course, not Enos Mills himself. Rather, it is an idealized, romanticized version of the kind of individual Mills would have liked to have been, shorn of all the complexities and rough edges that characterized the real man. Possessed with a contagious and endearing enthusiasm and a near childlike capacity for wonder, Mills's genial and mild-mannered narrator is a man incapable of sharp or unkind words. In Mills's public representation of himself, in short, there is certainly no hint of the choleric temperament or the rigid, inflexible mindset that all too often left him unwilling or unable to compromise on issues or to meet his opponents half-way.

Mills's narrator is, above all, a wise and generous guide to the wilderness, a latter-day version of the frontiersman, whose qualities, especially his self-reliance and rugged individualism, were widely associated in Mills's day as in our own with the quintessential American character. In place of this vanished American, Mills offered the attractive figure of the interpretive nature guide. "Our late lamented frontier is forever gone," Mills wrote, "and so, too, is the picturesque frontiersman, the trapper, the stage driver, and the audacious and heavily armed scout. The work of a guide is very much like that of a scout with shooting ability omitted and an array of nature information added. . . . there are numberless opportunities for helpful service and there will come frequent calls for heroic deeds."[59] Mills's nature guide, like Daniel Boone, Kit Carson, Davy Crockett and other worthies of the historic frontier, is pragmatic and resourceful, well-schooled in woodcraft and nature lore, and sufficient unto himself. He is a rather amiable eccentric, a basically shy and detached observer who courts the solitude of nature. "The characteristic thing in Mr. Mills's book," an earlier reviewer of *Wild Life on the Rockies* noted, "lies in the fact that it introduces to us quite a new sort of man—a man whose distinguishing quality is that his happiest days are those he spends in midwinter wandering over the highest slopes of the Rockies, with no other companion than his collie dog Scotch."[60] There is considerable truth in such judgments, for Enos Mills was unquestionably someone who often preferred to be alone.

As in the case with Mills's other early books, *Wild Life on the Rockies* consists for the most part of a series of independent essays organized around the narrator's adventures. They are bound together only by the general locale of their setting and by the narrator himself. Two of the fourteen essays—"The Story of a Thousand-Year Pine" and "Faithful Scotch"—became classics of the Mills canon, and were later republished separately in book form.

On the whole, the volume demonstrates Mills's strengths and weaknesses both as a writer and as a naturalist. As an author, his strengths clearly lie in his eye for detail, in his narrative ability, and in the simplicity and readability of his style. There is also his unmistakable talent as a frontier humorist, as for example in his tongue-in-chief retelling of the story of the two old-time prospectors Sullivan and Jason, who are besieged by bears in their cabin in Geneva Park. Among his most obvious weaknesses (weaknesses far more apparent in our time than in Mills's own), are the author's tendencies towards abstraction, didacticism, and sentimentality. Unquestionably, the optimistic Mills was also guilty of glossing over the darker side of nature. In part, such an omission was a matter of temperament—of what Mills himself wanted to see. But Mills also no doubt feared that unpleasant realities would detract from his basic message about the value of the outdoors and thus jeopardize his readers' growing support of wilderness preservation. Mills's choice of literary format was probably also somewhat unfortunate. Having begun his literary career as a writer for magazines, he remained, essentially, a writer of essays and articles, a fact that almost by definition limited the depth of treatment he could give his subject. His published volumes, with a few possible exceptions, were in this sense miscellanies rather than books.

When it comes to the nature content of his essays, Mills was on surer ground, and it was precisely to Mills's authenticity as a naturalist that his readers and listeners were drawn. "No student of natural history may say his library is complete," Arthur Weld of the *Waterloo Reporter* told his readers in November 1909, "if a copy of Enos A. Mills's *Wild Life in* [*sic*] *the Rockies* does not adorn the shelves. No book of recent issue, bearing on a similar subject, has attracted the widespread attention and favorable comment that this volume has."[61] What particularly attracted reviewers like Weld was Mills's keen powers of observation, which he reinforced by the use of his own photographs for illustrations. His nature lore—an amalgam of his own observations and his extensive reading in the leading authorities of the day—was substantial. So too were his achievements. Mills's *In Beaver World* (1913), for example, was the first important work on the animal since Lewis H. Morgan's study of 1865. Equally successful was his treatment of bears in *The Grizzly:*

Our Greatest Wild Animal (1919), in which Mills deliberately set out to correct long-standing myths and misconceptions about the grizzly that were leading to (and justifying) the extinction of a species that he considered "in most respects the greatest animal on the North American continent, if not the world."[62] Against the background of such obvious successes, it becomes foolish to quarrel unduly with Enos Mills's treatment of nature. There are shortcomings, to be sure, for at times Mills did not grasp the full complexity of some of the ecological issues he wrote about. But in this respect he did far better (and certainly did no worse) than most of his naturalist contemporaries.

If there is a blemish on Mills's record as a naturalist—a blemish that might well have done far more damage to his reputation among his contemporaries than it did—it was his early tendency toward anthropomorphizing wild life. At least one reviewer of *Wild Life on the Rockies* commented, though not necessarily unfavorably, on Mills's willingness to attribute to beavers, to Midget the return horse, and to his beloved Scotch the capacity to think:

> Enos A. Mills, in his new book, *Wild Life on the Rockies,* has the temerity to say what he thinks about some animals he has known, both wild and tame, and does not hesitate to credit them with a limited amount of brains and reasons.
>
> These utterances, of course, put Mr. Mills in the "reason" school of American nature writers, as opposed to the "instinct" school of which John Burroughs, the Sage of Slabsides, is the official mouthpiece.
>
> And, worse than that, Mr. Mills's name has presumably already gone on the blacklist as a "nature faker" of the most reckless sort, for some of the things he tells are not of the kind that would be apt to happen at Slabsides.[63]

The reviewer's allusion is to the controversy initiated by the much-admired John Burroughs in the March 1903 pages of the *Atlantic Monthly,* where he indicted as "sham naturalists" writers who attempted to humanize and sentimentalize animals by attributing to them human traits, including reason, rather than anchoring their treatment squarely in the observed scientific "facts" of animal life.[64] The quarrel, which was waged for the most part in the very magazines in which Mills sought to place his articles, reached its climax in September 1907 when Theodore Roosevelt delivered up own assault entitled "Nature Fakers" in *Everybody's Magazine*. "The modern "nature faker,'" Roosevelt asserted, "is of course an object of derision to every scientist worthy of the name, to every real lover of the wilderness, to every true hunter or nature lover."[65] Though the debate was by no means one-sided, the entrance of someone of Roosevelt's stature and authority into the fray on behalf of a coalition of writers and artists that included John Burroughs, John Muir, and Frederick Remington drew a line to be crossed only at the risk of one's public standing. The *Inter Ocean* reviewer, interestingly enough, was apparently willing to suspend judgment in the case of Enos Mills: "Nevertheless, we wish to give Mr. Burroughs a word of friendly warning. When he takes his hand to punish Mr. Mills, let him go slow and take heed of what he may say. For here is a man who knows what he is writing about." Such a challenge to the established Burroughs no doubt flattered Mills, who had just seen his own first book issued by Houghton Mifflin, Burroughs' publisher. But while such public disputes might do for established authors, they were clearly not for a newcomer like Mills who was intent on building a national reputation as a wilderness authority. Whatever the reason, Mills's later writings display far less willingness to anthropomorphize wild life into "Mr. Skunk" and "Mrs. Woodpecker" and by the time he came to write his own essay on the subject, "An Open Season on Animal Stories,"[66] there can be little doubt in whose company Enos Mills wished to be counted.

Though almost three-quarters of a century has now passed since the death of Enos Mills, his books and articles remain interesting and important documents in the history of early twentieth-century American conservation. Mills was neither a profound thinker nor a gifted writer. Nevertheless, he was a determined and deeply committed man who was able to convey to others the adventure and excitement of his wilderness experience. That his writings are now largely neglected has, finally, less to do with Enos Mills himself or the intrinsic value of his work than it does with the vagaries of changing literary tastes. His achievements both as writer and wilderness champion are real and need little apology. Enos Mills of the Rockies could truly say with John Muir of the Sierras, "I have done the best I could to show forth the beauty, grandeur, and all-embracing usefulness of our wild mountain forest reservations and parks, with the view to inciting the people to come and enjoy them, and get them into their hearts, so that at length their preservation and right use might be made sure."[67]

Notes

1. Emerson E. Lynn, "The Minister's Son" (1959), in *The Scottage*, typescript copies in both the Rocky Mountain National Park Library and Estes Park Public Library, pp. 28–29.

2. Enos A. Mills, Sr., *Pleasanton Observer*, February 25, 1910. A brief autobiographical narrative written by the elder Mills was inserted in his 1910 obituary.

3. Quoted in Frank S. Harrison, "Enos A. Mills—A Father of National Parks," Enos Mills Papers, Western History Department, Denver Public Library. This collection, presented to the Denver Public Library by Mills's widow, consists of manuscripts, correspondence, speeches, biographical data, and clippings and articles by and about Enos Mills. Hereafter cited as the Enos Mills Papers.

4. Dunraven (1841–1926), a wealthy Irish lord, first visited Estes Park on a hunting expedition in late December 1872 and again in 1873 and 1874. Impressed by both the scenery (which the German-born artist Albert Bierstadt, whom he imported, was to paint in 1876) and by the abundance of elk, deer, and mountain sheep, Dunraven embarked on an ambitious, and apparently partially fraudulent, attempt to gain control of Estes Park for a private game preserve. Though the Earl did succeed in gaining title to some fifteen thousand acres, his grand design was thwarted by the opposition of local residents and an aroused Colorado press. Instead, he organized the Estes Park Company, Ltd. (or English Company, as it came to be known), which turned to raising registered Hereford cattle and catering to a growing trade in summer tourists at the English (or Estes Park) Hotel, opened in July 1877. The hotel operated until August 4, 1911, when it burned to the ground. The nearby cottage, which Dunraven built for himself the same year, remains. Dunraven's ownership lasted until 1907, when Freelan O. Stanley, the inventor of the famous Stanley Steamer, and his partner, Burton D. Sanborn, purchased the Earl's residual interests of some six thousand acres. To the extent that

it discouraged speculation and retarded development, Dunraven's role in the early history of Estes Park was fortuitous. "We all began to see," pioneer Abner Sprague noted some years later, "that the holding of so much of the Park by one company, even if it had been secured unlawfully, was the best thing for the place, particularly after it was proven that the place was only valuable because of its location and its attraction for lovers of the out-of-doors." Quoted in Dave Hicks, *Estes Park from the Beginning* (Denver: A-T-P Publishing Co., 1976), p. 47.

5. Elkanah Lamb is discussed later on. Abner Sprague (1850–1943) homesteaded in Moraine Park (or Willow Park, as it was then known) in 1875. That same year Horace Ferguson (1826–1912) established a homestead that came to be known as the Highlands, just north of Marys Lake, and Alexander Q. MacGregor (1845–96) took up a similar claim along Black Canyon Creek. William E. James (?–1895) established the beginnings of the Elkhorn Lodge on Fall River in 1877. Sprague sold his ranch in 1904; it was then operated as Stead's Ranch and Hotel until it was purchased by the National Park Service and razed in the early 1960s. The James lodge, where Enos Mills worked during the summer of 1884, still stands at the head of Elkhorn Avenue, the principal street of the town of Estes Park.

6. Enos Mills was related to Elkanah Lamb on both his mother's and father's side and the two families were closely connected for many years. The mother of Enos A. Mills, Sr., Sarah Moon (1805–62), and the mother of Elkanah Lamb, Elizabeth Moon (1807–87), were sisters. Sarah married Abijah Mills (b. 1800) on September 2, 1824; Elizabeth married Esau Lamb (1806–83) on June 15, 1826. At the time of the 1850 census, the Esau Lamb and Abijah Mills families occupied adjacent farms in Union Township, St. Joseph County, Indiana. About 1852 the two families in the company of other relatives moved to Dallas County, Iowa, and then, in the spring of 1857, they again moved together, this time to Linn County, Kansas. Enos Mills's mother was the daughter of Josiah Lamb (1817–62), another of Elkanah Lamb's first cousins, who also arrived from Iowa with the Lamb-Mills party in 1857. Elkanah Lamb accompanied Enos and Ann Mills to the Colorado gold fields in the summer of 1860. Lamb continued to live in Linn County until 1866, when he moved to a homestead in Saline County, Nebraska.

Relations between Enos Mills and Elkanah Lamb and his second wife, Jane Morger Lamb, were initially cordial. In June and July 1900 Mills accompanied Lamb on Mills's first and only trip abroad, which included a visit to the Paris Exposition. Mills subsequently wrote a brief and friendly introduction to Lamb's volume of autobiographical reminiscences, *Memories of the Past and Thoughts of the Future* (United Brethren Publishing

House, 1906), in which he noted: "Though rarely agreeing with him on any proposition, yet for years I have probably been his most intimate friend. . . . Together we have seen Europe, addressed audiences, driven cattle, and enjoyed mountains, music, and sunsets [pp. v–vi]." Shortly thereafter, however, Mills and Lamb came to a parting of the ways. The reasons are obscure, though at least one of their near neighbors, Charles Edwin Hewes (1870–1947), who came to Estes Park in 1907 and for the next forty years ran Hewes-Kirkwood Inn, was inclined to credit it to a "confirmed egotism" resulting from Enos Mills's growing regional and national reputation. "He refuses to conform to any opinion save his own," Hewes noted in a journal entry of January 1, 1914, "and it is quite impossible to persuade, suggest, or present anything different." (Journal of Charles Edwin Hewes, January 1, 1914, p. 173.) Hewes faithfully kept this remarkable 1,116-page journal from 1913 to 1944. The unpublished typewritten manuscript, which was discovered together with Hewes's equally remarkable autobiography in an Estes Park bank vault, is the property of the Estes Park Area Historical Museum. Hereafter cited as Hewes Journal.) The quarrel between the two men, in its public manifestations at least, seems to have been petty. Lamb, like Hewes, was a member of a small group of Longs Peak Valley residents who banded together as the Front Range Settlers League to oppose Mills's proposal for a new national park; Mills, on his part, stubbornly opposed "for personal reasons" the attempt by Hewes and others to persuade the Colorado Geographic Board to change the name of Longs Peak Valley (subsequently Tahosa Valley) to Elkanah Valley in honor of Parson Lamb, "saying that the name had no particular connection with the valley." (Harriet Vail, secretary of the Colorado Geographic Board, quoted in Louisa Ward Arps and Elinor Eppich Kingery, *High Country Names* [Estes Park: Rocky Mountain Nature Assoc., 1972], p. 186.)

Charles Hewes, for one, saw the irony of the situation:

> Whenever any one criticizes him [Lamb] to his [Mills's] character, and upon one occasion when Mills reported him to the Government for stealing wood and for piling brush near the State road placed there thirty-five years previous to Mill's report when Mr. Lamb made the first road into this country [i.e., in 1875–76], Mr. Lamb always pulls down one of these books [*Memories of the Past and Thoughts of the Future,* in which Lamb had referred to "my friend, Enos A. Mills"] from the shelf and points to Mill's endorsement of him, it usually resulting in the reader's amused smile and the immediate cessation of all hostilities. Be the truth known, Mills loss of the friendship and esteem of Mr. and Mrs. Lamb is, to my eyes at

least, a frightful calamity, and can only be explained by inexplicable change of character since his absurd egotism led him estray [sic]. He has himself told me that he received the first inspiration and the love of nature things at Mr. Lamb's fireside when he first came into this vale a little fellow in skirts. It was Mr. Lamb and wife who first induced him to venture into the lecture field, they celebrated the event with a fine public dinner given in his behalf. Mrs. Lamb has served him countless meals, lunches, and goodies. . . .

(Hewes Journal, March 4, 1913, p. 35.)

Such quarrels die hard. There is no mention of the Mills-Lamb relationship in *Enos Mills of the Rockies* (New York: Junior Literary Guild and Houghton Mifflin, 1935), the appreciative biography that Mills's widow, Esther Burnell Mills, and Hildegarde Hawthorne collaborated on in 1935. Interestingly enough, their biography contains only a single reference to Enos's younger brother, Enoch "Joe" Mills (1880–1935), with whom Enos also quarreled and parted company. The two brothers had been closely identified during the early years of the Longs Peak Inn. Joe later ran a successful mountain resort in Estes Park. The relationship between Enos and Joe Mills is discussed in my introduction to Joe Mills's *A Mountain Boyhood* (1926; reprint, Lincoln: University of Nebraska Press, 1988).

7. *Memories of the Past,* p. 166.

8. Enos A. Mills, *Loveland Reporter,* vol. 23, August 14, 1902, p. 1. Enos Mills Papers.

9. Enos A. Mills, "Who's Who—and Why: Enos A. Mills Himself, By Himself," *Saturday Evening Post* (September 1, 1917): 9.

10. Undated letter, Enos Mills Papers.

11. Enos A. Mills, *Waiting in the Wilderness* (Garden City, N.Y.: Doubleday, Page and Co., 1921), p. 93.

12. Undated autobiographical essay, Enos Mills Papers.

13. Letter of January 31, 1913. Muir-Mills Correspondence, Pacific Center for Western Historical Studies, University of the Pacific, Stockton, California.

14. *Literary Digest* (July 14, 1917). Quoted in Stephen Fox, *John Muir and His Legacy: The American Conservation Movement* (Boston: Little, Brown and Co., 1981), p. 121.

15. Carlyle Lamb (1862–1958), eight years Mills's senior, arrived in Estes Park with Elkanah Lamb in 1875 and became a junior partner in the Longs Peak House venture. Carlyle first ascended Longs Peak with his father, mother, and brother in 1879. He became a guide in 1880 and for the next twenty-two years made some 146 trips to the summit. It was in this capacity that Carlyle Lamb introduced both Frederick Chapin and Enos

Mills to the spectacular views from the top of Longs Peak. It was Carlyle Lamb rather than his father who in 1889 actually secured formal title to the 160-acre tract at the base of Longs Peak on which Longs Peak House stood. Following the sale of the property to Enos Mills, the Lambs built a new ranch called Mountain Home some two miles to the north at the head of Wind River, a place long known as Lamb's Notch (the current site of Wind River Ranch).

16. M. Kennedy Bailey, "A Forest House," *The Craftsman*, 20 (May 1911): 205.

17. *Estes Park Trail,* vol. 3, August 15, 1914, p. 9.

18. "A Few Day's Outing," *Estes Park Trail,* vol. 1, September 28, 1912, p. 5.

19. Lynn, "The Minister's Son," p. 29.

20. Papers of J. Horace McFarland, File 80, Division of Public Records, Pennsylvania Historical Museum Commission, Harrisburg, Pennsylvania. This collection contains correspondence between Enos Mills and J. Horace McFarland (1859–1948), the president of the American Civic Association, as well as other assorted materials, including this poem, covering the period 1910 to 1921. Hereafter cited as McFarland Papers.

21. Enos Mills Papers.

22. Quoted in Harold R. Steen, *The U. S. Forest Service: A History* (Seattle: University of Washington Press, 1976), p. 86.

23. Unsigned rev., *Daily Independent,* May 12, 1907, Enos Mills Papers.

24. Unsigned rev., Enos Mills Papers.

25. Carl Abbott, "The Active Force: Enos A. Mills and the National Park Movement," *Colorado Magazine,* 56 (1979): 60.

26. Mills, "Who's Who—and Why," p. 25.

27. In May 1905, Roosevelt extended Wyoming's Medicine Bow Forest Preserve southward to include the wilderness area now embraced by Rocky Mountain National Park, a decision that led in 1907 to the establishment of a local Forest Service headquarters at Estes Park under the direction of H. N. Wheeler, the newly appointed chief of the Medicine Bow Reserve. (In 1910 the section of the Medicine Bow Forest Reserve in Colorado was renamed the Colorado National Forest, a name that lasted until 1932 when it was changed to the current Roosevelt National Forest.) The Estes Park Protective and Improvement Association, an informal forum in which to air and resolve community issues, was founded in 1906. Its president was Freelan O. Stanley (1849–1940), who in 1907, together with his partner, Burton D. Sanborn of Greeley, purchased the Earl of Dunraven's remaining holdings (see n. 4, above) and a year later began construction of the luxurious Stanley Hotel, which opened its doors in June 1909. The Association's secretary was Cornelius H. Bond (1854–

1931). It was Bond, together with four partners, who in March 1905 purchased, surveyed, subdivided, and offered for sale the original 160-acre homestead at the confluence of the Big Thompson and Fall rivers that became the site of the town of Estes Park.

28. Quoted in C. W. Bucholtz, *Rocky Mountain National Park: A History* (Boulder: Colorado Associated University Press, 1983), p. 132. The most detailed account of the campaign that created Rocky Mountain National Park is found in Patricia M. Fazio, "Cragged Crusade: The Fight for Rocky Mountain National Park, 1909–1915," master's thesis, University of Wyoming, Laramie, 1982. For other accounts, see Bucholtz, pp. 126–37, and Lloyd K. Musselman, *Rocky Mountain National Park: Administrative History, 1915–1965* (Washington: U. S. Department of the Interior, National Park Service, 1971), pp. 17–27.

29. Enos A. Mills, *The Rocky Mountain National Park* (Garden City, N.Y.: Doubleday, Page and Co, 1924), p. 86.

30. The tension between those who would judiciously use the wilderness for the utilitarian needs of civilization and those who would preserve it untouched for its spiritual and aesthetic values has been at the center of the American conservation movement from the very beginning. As Roderick Nash notes, John Muir himself for a time "tried to keep a foot in both camps, recognizing the claims of both the wilderness and civilization to the American landscape. . . . After a period of vacillation and confusion, Muir ended, inevitably, by opting for the preservationist interpretation of conservation, while others followed Gifford Pinchot and the professional foresters into the 'wise use' school." See Roderick Nash, *Wilderness and the American Mind* (New Haven: Yale University Press, 1967), pp. 129–30. As the accounts of his public lectures indicate, Enos Mills also seems to have tried initially to straddle the issue. In order to win new supporters for the conservation movement, Mills had to convince his listeners that forests were important to the future economic well-being of American civilization and that they had become imperiled by decades of unrestricted use and exploitation. Though he talked about the spiritual and aesthetic value of forests, Mills's essential message was one that at least implicitly assumed wise usage in general accord with the Pinchot formulation. Like John Muir, Enos Mills eventually had to make a choice.

31. Mills's quarrel with the Forest Service began in earnest in late December 1910 or early January 1911, when it came to his attention that members of the Forest Service were arguing that "a game preserve," under its control, would best serve the needs and interests of Estes Park because a national park "will lock up the resources of the region." Having openly complained of the Service's opposition to scenic preservation ("Scratch any old Forest Service man," he wrote McFarland on March 20,

1911, "and you will find a Tartar who is opposed to all National Parks"), Mills came to believe that the Forest Service was not only out to discredit him but to harass him by allowing cattle to graze on his property and along the Longs Peak trail to the detriment of mountain climbers, many of whom were guests at the Inn (a charge that Chief Forester Henry Graves himself personally investigated and vigorously denied). By late 1914 his insistence that an "aggressive" conspiratorial Forest Service was using every means "to suppress and blackmail into silence any opposition to its methods" had become so intemperate that McFarland warned him in a letter of December 28 that "your splendid work is being discounted because of the hostility toward the Forest Service. . . . I do not trust the Forest Service any more than you do, but I do not want to let my feeling in that direction handicap the possibility of doing something for the National parks" (McFarland Papers).

The deterioration of Mills's relationship with Denver lawyer James Grafton Rogers (1883–1971), who worked diligently on behalf of the national park idea as founding president of the Colorado Mountain Club, was even more unfortunate. The campaign for the establishment of the new park was finally a political one in which success depended on the willingness to compromise. As Rogers told Mills in a letter of February 6, 1913, "In order to unite all these various interests, we had to make a number of concessions in the way of mining rights, water rights, and so on, but I think that these are all details which can be overlooked in the general success of the project" (quoted in Abbott, "The Active Force," p. 63). Rogers accepted the reality of compromise; Enos Mills did not. Upset by such decisions and by the inevitable delay of getting his park bill through the Congress, Mills unfairly took out his frustration on Rogers, accusing him of hypocritically "conniving with the Forest Service" and of being "the greatest opponent that the Park has" (McFarland Papers). As Abbott observes, "In the world of Enos Mills, anyone who was not an active supporter was a potential enemy, compromise with rival interests was betrayal, and bureaucratic organization was an impediment to the quick achievement of self-evident goals" ("The Active Force," p. 72).

32. Marshall's instructions from Secretary of the Interior Walter L. Fisher were verbal and open-ended: "Go out and see what you can and come back and tell me about it" (quoted in Fazio, p. 136). His report of January 9, 1913, recommending the establishment of a park consisting of some seven hundred square miles (450,450 acres) was enthusiastic. "Taking all things into consideration," he wrote, "it is my opinion that the creation and maintenance of a national park in this section of the Rocky Mountains is not only feasible but highly desirable and that every effort should be made to secure the establishment of such a park at the earliest

practicable date." Robert B. Marshall, "Report on an Examination of the Area of the Proposed Rocky Mountain (Estes) National Park, Colorado," January 9, 1913, Records of the Office of the Secretary of the Interior, R. G. 79, National Archives.

33. In 1917 Rocky Mountain National Park was expanded to include Gem Lake, Deer Mountain, and Twin Sisters Mountain. It was enlarged again in 1929 to include the Never Summer Range to the west, and now encompasses some 412 square miles.

34. Fazio, "Cragged Crusade," p. 177. See, for example, Enos A. Mills, "A New National Park," *Saturday Evening Post* (March 5, 1910): 60, and Enos A. Mills, "The Proposed Estes National Park," *Sierra Club Bulletin,* 7 (June 1910): 234–35. The second article featured four of Mills's own photographs.

35. Quoted in Fazio, "Cragged Crusade," p. 134.

36. Mills to McFarland, April 24, 1912, McFarland Papers.

37. Enos Mills File, Rocky Mountain National Park Library.

38. Gifford Pinchot and his successor, Henry Graves, were enormously successful in establishing new forest reserves and in publicizing the virtues of their wise-use approach to forestry. They also, ironically, convinced strict preservationists like Enos Mills that the Forest Service was not to be trusted with the management of the nation's parks. As a result, by 1910 Mills and his colleagues had come to view a separate park bureau as absolutely essential if their own preservationist goals were to be met. Mills made the need for such a bureau one of his lecture themes and for a time was part of a small coterie of nature enthusiasts who met in Washington in early 1916 to plan the strategy leading to the legislation that created the National Park Service. In January 1917, following the passage of the Park Service bill, Mills attended the National Parks Conference in Washington, where he presided over a session discussing the recreational use of national parks. Several months later he published *Your National Parks,* "an ambitious volume recognized by reviewers as the standard introduction to the new park service." Abbott, "The Active Force," p. 63. See also Robert Shankland, *Steve Mather of the National Parks* (New York: Alfred A. Knopf, 1951), p. 101.

39. Quoted in Peter J. Schmitt, *Back to Nature: The Arcadian Myth in Urban America* (New York: Oxford University Press, 1969), p. 162.

40. Ronald A. Foresta, *America's National Parks and Their Keepers* (Washington, D.C.: Resources for the Future, Inc., 1984), p. 24.

41. The transportation concessions controversy from Enos Mills's point of view is recounted in Mills and Hawthorne's *Enos Mills of the Rockies,* pp. 223–51. For another account, which is not without its Park Service biases, see Musselman's *Rocky Mountain National Park,* pp. 29–76. Though the

new concessions policy provided the occasion for a full-scale battle with
the National Park Service, relations between Mills and the new agency
were already strained and Mills, on his part, had decided, as early apparently as the summer of 1917, that administrators like Mather and his
assistant Horace Albright not only were not being aggressive enough in
their support of Rocky Mountain National Park but in fact were guilty of
using their official positions "to screen the insidious work of the Forest
Service." Albright, in particular, he denounced as "a menace to the entire
cause of the National Parks" (quoted in Donald C. Swain, *Wilderness De-
fender: Horace M. Albright and Conservation* [Chicago: University of Chicago Press, 1970] pp. 86, 94). See also Horace M. Albright, *The Birth of the
National Park Service: The Founding Years, 1913–1933* (Salt Lake City: Howe
Brothers, 1985), p. 62.

42. Mills to McFarland, March 17, 1914, McFarland Papers.

43. Mills to McFarland, October 6, 1920, McFarland Papers.

44. Quoted in Musselman, *Rocky Mountain National Park,* p. 36.

45. The series of inconclusive court cases reached their climax in January 1926, when the State of Colorado, threatened with the loss of major
federal appropriations for road maintenance and construction within the
park, dropped the litigation. This placed the issue squarely in the hands
of the Colorado legislature, which was called upon to debate a bill ceding
to the federal government final jurisdiction over all state roads within the
park. The high drama that ensued, which fully engaged the attention of
the state press and brought forth lobbying groups up and down the Front
Range, was filled with heated accusations of government intimidation and
federal "encroachment on the rights and property of States." The issue
continued to be contested until February 1929, when political fervor gave
way to economic realities—in the form of some $500,000 in federal road
appropriations—and the cede bill was passed by both legislative houses
and signed into law. The purely legal aspects of the cede jurisdiction dis-
pute are found in William Sherman Bell, "The Legal Phases of Cession
of Rocky Mountain National Park," *Rocky Mountain Law Review,* 1 (1928):
35–46. The public controversy is well documented in two scrapbooks
containing clippings on the cede jurisdiction bill that are part of the per-
manent collection of the Rocky Mountain National Park Library.

Enos Mills had what James Grafton Rogers referred to as "a genius for
making enemies" and, he might have added, of alienating even his most
admiring friends and supporters. This unfortunate facet of Mills's personality was clearly evident in his battle with the Park Service and its
concessions policy, which virtually severed his relationship of more than
a decade with J. Horace McFarland. McFarland, as noted above, had become increasingly wary of Mills's outbursts and tried on various occa-

sions to get him to see that his tactics were counterproductive. By 1920 their relationship had reached the breaking point. "I think your course tends toward the belief that you are somewhat unbalanced," he told Mills bluntly on September 25, 1920. "Certainly you are losing influence, which is unfortunate. All this slop about Prussian invaders, transportation monopolies, and other things you do not like, does nothing for you and only discredits the parks you really love. Can't you cut it out Mr. Mills?" Mills lashed back: "I learned years ago," he told McFarland on October 6, 1920, "that the President of the American Civic Association, though once a fighter, was not likely to campaign against the powers-that-be." Despite what Mills believed to be incontrovertible facts, the public remained ignorant about "profiteering" in the parks. "As for yourself," Mills concluded, "I doubt if you even want to know."

The long-suffering McFarland was plainly stung. "Not a word you say is constructive," he responded to Mills a week later, on October 11, 1920.

> You are campaigning to break them down [the Forest and Park services], without any apparent plan to better the situation. The success of your endeavors would be heralded with joy by the power interests, by the irrigation interests, by the lumber interests. . . . Mr. Mills, you are dead wrong in your attitude and are losing not only the opportunity to extend the great work you have already done but to be regarded seriously by worth-while people by your violence . . . . You cannot possibly maintain as one single American that you are always right and everyone you criticize always wrong, nor can you possibly sustain an attitude of continuous objurgation and scolding with any expectation that you will be taken seriously. (McFarland Papers)

Nor was McFarland the only one to worry about the consequences of what Mills was doing. On May 27, 1921, Mills took his case against the Park Service to the Denver Civic and Commercial Association in the form of an address. Because of the seriousness of the charges and the danger they posed to the Colorado tourist industry, the Board of Directors appointed a special committee to look into Mills's allegations. Although Mills declined to substantiate his charges, the committee mounted an exhaustive investigation: it "examined the original records at Washington, D.C.; . . . corresponded with all parties who . . . possessed any knowledge as to the facts in the case; . . . read many resolutions, letters, and published articles bearing on the subject and in every way . . . [went] into the matter thoroughly and impartially with the intention of enabling the members of this Association to reach a just conclusion and a business-like determination." Their report, which was unanimously adopted by the Board on November 3, 1921, was devastating. The committee took no position on the legality of an exclusive franchise agreement: that was a question for the federal courts to decide. But as far as Mills's other assertions were concerned, it minced no words: "Everyone of the specific charges made by Enos Mills has not only been disproven but no facts have been found that would tend to furnish a foundation for any one of the charges." Mills's conduct was "decidedly reprehensible," his speech filled with "vituperation, vindictiveness, fabrication, [and] deliberately misleading statements and untruths." Particularly damaging to Mills's credibility was the statement, "It is illuminating when considering the present opposition of Mills to the granting of transportation franchises in National Parks to note that on November 7, 1919, he made application for the granting of such a franchise to himself: 'over all the roads within Rocky Mountain National Park.'" A copy of the Association's report is part of the McFarland Papers.

46. For all his suspicion of commercial interests, Enos Mills himself was a shrewd businessman. In July 1914, anticipating the establishment of Rocky Mountain National Park and the influx of new visitors, Mills purchased the eighty-acre turn-of-the-century homestead property of local artist Richard Tallant (d. 1932), located on the rim of Devils Gulch on the road to Glen Haven northeast of the village of Estes Park. "The old homestead," the *Estes Park Trail* reported, "has been fitted up as a dining room and kitchen, with a veranda looking down the Park, and a number of cottages furnish comfortable rooms for guests." Mills christened his new establishment "The Horizon" because "with the great expanse of the Park to the south . . . [it enjoyed] a magnificent view of Long's Peak and the Snowy range in the background." *Estes Park Trail*, vol. 3, July 25, 1914, p. 10. The enterprising Mills apparently was not through, for the same story noted that "Mr. Mills is making plans for a new hotel which he expects to build before another season, and make it second only to Long's Peak Inn as a popular resort for visitors to the Park." Mills may have planned his new hotel for Horseshoe Park, a flat picturesque valley located well within the boundaries projected for the new park, for Charles Hewes noted in a September 1914 journal entry that Mills had recently purchased two hundred acres there (Hewes Journal, May-September 1914, p. 231). The same journal entry also indicates that Mills had recently opened a restaurant in Estes Park Village. Interestingly enough, it was also in 1914 that Joe Mills, Enos's estranged younger brother, built and opened "The Crags" hotel on the side of Prospect Mountain close to the village.

47. Esther Burnell Mills, who like her husband was born in Kansas, was

the daughter of the Reverend Arthur Burnell. Educated at Lake Erie
College and at Pratt Institute, her career as an interior decorator for
Sherwin-Williams was interrupted by the nervous breakdown that
brought her to Longs Peak Inn in the summer of 1916, along with her
sister Elizabeth. (She had apparently attended a Mills lecture in Cleveland the preceding year.) At the end of the season, during which Esther
did some part-time secretarial work for Mills, Elizabeth returned to
teaching in California, while Esther herself took up a homestead off Fall
River Road near Castle Mountain just west of the village of Estes Park.
She named her homestead cabin, of which she took formal title in 1918,
"Keewaydin" after the Indian name for the Northwest or home wind. Mills
wrote an appreciative essay about his wife entitled "Evolution of a Woman
Guide," which he included in *The Adventures of a Nature Guide* (1920).

Following her husband's death in 1922, Esther Mills ran Longs Peak
Inn until 1945, when she sold it and moved to a small house not far from
Enos's homestead cabin. Old-time visitors noted the difference. With Enos
Mills's death, Emerson Lynn recalled, "Long's Peak Inn lost its unique and
piquant flavor. . . . Mrs. Mills wished to maintain the Inn as a memorial
to her husband. She kept it austere, but made it somber and vapid, slowly
smothering it to death" (Lynn, p. 29). Longs Peak Inn burned to the
ground in 1946. Enos Mills's original 1885–86 homestead cabin across
the road remains. Containing his books, pictures, and other memorabi-
lia, it is operated as a museum by his daughter, Enda Mills Kiley, and her
husband.

48. Mills and Hawthorne, *Enos Mills of the Rockies*, p. 245.

49. Hewes Journal, p. 543.

50. Ibid., p. 544.

51. Enos Mills Papers, May 22, 1922.

52. Hewes Journal, p. 545.

53. *Estes Park Trail*, vol. 2, September 22, 1922, p. 1. Though the death
certificate, signed by a Longmont dentist, gives "myocardial-infarction"
(a heart attack) as the cause of Mills's death, it is probable that it was
brought on by blood poisoning resulting from the abscess.

54. Lynn, "The Minister's Son," pp. 28–29.

55. *The Denver Post*, September 25, 1922. Emerson Lynn, who was man-
aging the Inn at the time of Mills's death and was deputed by Mrs. Mills
to make the required funeral arrangements, recalled "the beautiful sunset which did fill the western sky just as the body was lowered into the
grave" (Lynn, "The Minister's Son," p. 29). A more prosaic account appeared the following Friday in the *Estes Park Trail*, vol. 2, September 29,
1922, p. 1. A year later Esther Mills, apparently fearing that Mills's grave
might be desecrated by vandals, had her husband's body exhumed and

cremated in Denver. His ashes were returned to Longs Peak and scattered. *Denver Post,* June 1, 1923, p. 1; June 3, 1923, p. 2.

56. Enos Mills Papers.

57. During the last year of his life, as Carl Abbott notes, Mills gained surer control over both his style and subject matter and became "a better and more interesting writer." Mills's observations of nature became more precise and detailed, and there were fewer attempts at overdramatization, elaborate comparison, and cuteness. In addition, Mills curbed his earlier tendency to humanize his animal subjects. Carl Abbott, "The Literary Career of Enos Mills," *Montana: The Magazine of Western History,* 31 (April 1981): 2–15. Mills's abilities as a writer and naturalist are also discussed in Peter Wild, *Enos Mills* (Boise: Boise State University, 1979).

58. M. E. Cook, rev. of *Wild Life on the Rockies, Dial,* 46 (June 1, 1909): 363.

59. Mills, *Rocky Mountain National Park,* p. 158.

60. Unsigned rev., April 24, 1909, Enos Mills Papers.

61. Arthur Weld, *Waterloo Reporter,* November 6, 1909, Enos Mills Papers.

62. Enos A. Mills, *The Grizzly: Our Greatest Wild Animal* (Boston: Houghton Mifflin Company, 1919), p. ix.

63. Unsigned and undated rev., *Inter Ocean,* Enos Mills Papers.

64. John Burroughs, "Real and Sham Naturalists," *Atlantic Monthly,* 91 (March 1903): 298–309.

65. Theodore Roosevelt, "Nature Fakers," *Everybody's Magazine,* 17 (September 1907): 428. See also Paul Russell Cutright, "The Nature Faker Controversy," *Theodore Roosevelt the Naturalist* (New York: Harper and Brothers, 1956), pp. 126–39.

66. Mills, *Waiting in the Wilderness,* pp. 209–25.

67. Muir, *Our National Parks,* Preface.

Enos A. Mills: A Chronology

1870   April 22, Enos Abijah Mills born.

1884   Journeys to Estes Park, Colorado, by way of Kansas City and Denver. Works at Elkhorn Lodge.

1885   Works at Elkanah Lamb's Longs Peak House. First ascent of Longs Peak guided by Carlyle Lamb. Begins work on homestead cabin. Spends winter working on ranch in eastern Colorado.

1886   Works again for Lambs. Helps Carlyle Lamb construct Longs Peak trail. Completes cabin.

1887   Summer in Estes Park. First solo ascent of Longs Peak. Travels to Butte, Montana, to work as tool boy at Anaconda copper mine.

1888   Summer in Estes Park. Promoted to miner at Butte.

1889   Guides first party to summit of Longs Peak. Fall, fire closes Anaconda mine. December, meets John Muir in San Francisco.

1890   Visits Death Valley, Yosemite, Sequoias, Virginia City and Reno; explores California coast south to San Diego. September, enrolls in Heald's Business College in San Francisco.

1891   January, returns to Butte to assume office position, but soon resigns. Spring, explores Yellowstone; remains for summer working with U.S. Geological Survey party.

1892   Spring, visits Alaska.

1893   Works in Ward, Colorado. Visits Chicago World's Fair and family in Kansas.

1894   Revisits Alaska. Deserted by guides, Mills walks alone more than two hundred miles from north of Chilcoot Pass south to Juneau.

1895   Fall, makes first forestry speech in Kansas City.

1896   February, addresses teachers' convention in Linn County, Kansas, and receives twenty-five dollars. Begins reporting Estes Park resort news for Denver newspapers.

1896–   Spends winter working in mines at Victor and Cripple
1897   Creek.

1900   June 6, sails for Southampton to visit Paris Exposition with Elkanah Lamb. Visits Switzerland, Venice, Florence, Rome, and England. Sails for home on July 14.

1902   Purchases Longs Peak House from Carlyle Lamb. Publishes first magazine article in *Outdoor Life*. Scotch arrives as puppy.

1902–   December-January, as snow observer completes six-
1903   day, 120-mile walk inspecting headwaters of the South Platte.

1903   February, makes first winter climb of Longs Peak, and journeys across Flattop Mountain to Grand Lake. June, repeats Elkanah Lamb's 1871 descent of East Face of Longs Peak. October, visits Mesa Verde.

1904   February, as snow observer completes seventy-mile trip inspecting headwaters of Grand, Big Thompson, and Michigan rivers.

1905   *The Story of Estes Park and a Guide Book* published. Fall-winter, undertakes eighty-lecture tour of East, including Kansas City, Memphis, New Orleans, Pittsburg, Columbus, Chicago.

1906   June, main building of Longs Peak Inn burns while
        Enos is lecturing in St. Paul. Completes his last season
        as a Longs Peak guide. Makes thirty-two ascents during
        month of August. Lectures extensively. Meets John
        Burroughs.

1907   January, accepts Roosevelt's invitation to become spe-
        cial Government Lecturer on Forestry.

1908   Builds Timberline House on Longs Peak Trail, halfway
        to summit.

1909   May, resigns as Government Lecturer. *Wild Life on the
        Rockies* published. Fall, begins to campaign actively for a
        new national park in Estes Park area.

1910   June, Scotch is accidentally killed trying to extinguish
        the fuse on a charge of dynamite being used by a road
        crew near Longs Peak Inn.

1911   *The Spell of the Rockies* published.

1913   *In Beaver World* published.

1914   *The Story of a Thousand-Year Pine* published.

1915   January 16, Rocky Mountain National Park created by
        act of Congress. September 5, Park dedicated, with
        Enos Mills as master of ceremonies. *Rocky Mountain
        Wonderland* published.

1916   Enlarges Longs Peak Inn. *The Story of Scotch* published.

1917   January, attends National Parks Conference in Wash-
        ington, presides at session discussing "The Recreational
        Use of National Parks." *Your National Parks* published.

1918   Marries Esther Burnell (1889–1946) on August 12 in
        ceremony at homestead cabin.

1919   Enda Mills born on April 27. Transportation conces-
        sions controversy begins. *Being Good to Bears: And Other
        True Animal Stories* and *The Grizzly: Our Greatest Wild An-
        imal* published.

1920   *The Adventures of a Nature Guide* published.

1921   *Waiting in the Wilderness* published.

1922   January, injured in New York City subway collision. Enos Mills dies on September 22. *Watched by Wild Animals* published.

1923   *Wild Animal Homesteads* published.

1924   *The Rocky Mountain National Park* published.

1926   *Romance of Geology* published.

1931   *Bird Memories of the Rockies* published.

Preface

THIS book contains the record of a few of the many happy days and novel experiences which I have had in the wilds. For more than twenty years it has been my good fortune to live most of the time with nature, on the mountains of the West. I have made scores of long exploring rambles over the mountains in every season of the year, a nature-lover charmed with the birds and the trees. On my later excursions I have gone alone and without firearms. During three succeeding winters, in which I was a Government Experiment Officer and called the "State Snow Observer," I scaled many of the higher peaks of the Rockies and made many studies on the upper slopes of these mountains.

"Colorado Snow Observer" was printed in part in *The Youth's Companion* for May 18, 1905, under the title of "In the Mountain Snows"; "The Story of a Thousand-Year Pine"

Preface

appeared in *The World's Work* for August, 1908; and "The Beaver and his Works" is reprinted from *The World To-Day* for December, 1908.

E. A. M.

Colorado Snow Observer

Colorado Snow Observer

WHERE are you going?" was the question asked me one snowy winter day. After hearing that I was off on a camping-trip, to be gone several days, and that the place where I intended to camp was in deep snow on the upper slopes of the Rockies, the questioners laughed heartily. Knowing me, some questioners realized that I was in earnest, and all that they could say in the nature of argument or appeal was said to cause me to "forego the folly." But I went, and in the romance of a new world—on the Rockies in winter—I lived intensely through ten strong days and nights, and gave to my life new and rare experiences. Afterwards I made other winter excursions, all of which were stirring and satisfactory. The recollection of these winter experiences is as complete and exhilarating as any in the vista of my memory.

Some years after my first winter camping-trip, I found myself holding a strange position,—that

3

of the "State Snow Observer of Colorado." I
have never heard of another position like it. Professor L. G. Carpenter, the celebrated irrigation
engineer, was making some original investiga-
tions concerning forests and the water-supply.
He persuaded me to take the position, and under
his direction I worked as a government experiment officer. For three successive winters I
traversed the upper slopes of the Rockies and
explored the crest of the continent, alone. While
on this work, I was instructed to make notes on
"those things that are likely to be of interest or
value to the Department of Agriculture or the
Weather Bureau," — and to be careful not to
lose my life.

On these winter trips I carried with me a camera, thermometer, barometer, compass, notebook,
and folding axe. The food carried usually was
only raisins. I left all bedding behind. Notwithstanding I was alone and in the wilds, I did not
carry any kind of a gun.

The work made it necessary for me to ramble
the wintry heights in sunshine and storm. Often
I was out, or rather up, in a blizzard, and on

more than one occasion I was out for two weeks
on the snow-drifted crest of the continent, without
seeing any one. I went beyond the trails and visited the silent places alone. I invaded gulches,
eagerly walked the splendid forest aisles, wan-
dered in the dazzling glare on dreary alpine
moorlands, and scaled the peaks over mantles of
ice and snow. I had many experiences, — amusing, dangerous, and exciting. There was abundance of life and fun in the work. On many an
evening darkness captured me and compelled
me to spend the night in the wilds without
bedding, and often without food. During these
nights I kept a camp-fire blazing until daylight
released me. When the night was mild, I managed to sleep a little, — in installments, — rising
from time to time to give wood to the eager fire.
Sometimes a scarcity of wood kept me busy gathering it all night; and sometimes the night was so
cold that I did not risk going to sleep. During
these nights I watched my flaming fountain of
fire brighten, fade, surge, and change, or shower
its spray of sparks upon the surrounding snow-
flowers. Strange reveries I have had by these

winter camp-fires. On a few occasions mountain lions interrupted my thoughts with their piercing, lonely cries; and more than once a reverie was pleasantly changed by the whisper of a chickadee in some near-by tree as a cold comrade snuggled up to it. Even during the worst of nights, when I thought of my lot at all. I considered it better than that of those who were sick in houses or asleep in the stuffy, deadly air of the slums.

> " Believe me, 't is something to be cast
> Face to face with thine own self at last."

Not all nights were spent outdoors. Many a royal evening was passed in the cabin of a miner or a prospector, or by the fireside of a family who for some reason had left the old home behind and sought seclusion in wild scenes, miles from neighbors. Among Colorado's mountains there are an unusual number of strong characters who are trying again. They are strong because broken plans, lost fortunes, or shattered health elsewhere have not ended their efforts or changed their ideals. Many are trying to restore health, some are trying again to prosper, others are just making a start in

A MAN WITH A HISTORY

life, but there are a few who, far from the madding crowd, are living happily the simple life. Sincerity, hope, and repose enrich the lives of those who live among the crags and pines of mountain fastnesses. Many a happy evening I have had with a family, or an old prospector, who gave me interesting scraps of autobiography along with a lodging for the night.

The snow-fall on the mountains of Colorado is very unevenly distributed, and is scattered through seven months of the year. Two places only a few miles apart, and separated by a mountain-range, may have very different climates, and one of these may have twice as much snow-fall as the other. On the middle of the upper slopes of the mountains the snow sometimes falls during seven months of the year. At an altitude of eleven thousand feet the annual fall amounts to eighteen feet. This is several times the amount that falls at an altitude of six thousand feet. In a locality near Crested Butte the annual fall is thirty feet, and during snowy winters even fifty feet. Most winter days are clear, and the climate less severe than is usually imagined.

Wild Life on the Rockies

One winter I walked on snowshoes on the upper slopes of the "snowy" range of the Rockies, from the Wyoming line on the north to near the New Mexico line on the south. This was a long walk, and it was full of amusement and adventure. I walked most of the way on the crest of the continent. The broken nature of the surface gave me ups and downs. Sometimes I would descend to the level of seven thousand feet, and occasionally I climbed some peak that was fourteen thousand feet above the tides.

I had not been out many days on this trip when I was caught in a storm on the heights above tree-line. I at once started downward for the woods. The way among the crags and precipices was slippery; the wind threatened every moment to hurl me over a cliff; the wind-blown snow filled the air so that I could see only a few feet, and at times not at all. But it was too cold to stop. For two hours I fought my way downward through the storm, and so dark was it during the last half-hour that I literally felt my way with my staff. Once in the woods, I took off a snowshoe, dug a large hole in the snow down to

the earth, built a fire, and soon forgot the perilous descent. After eating from my supply of raisins, I dozed a little, and woke to find all calm
and the moon shining in glory on a snowy moun-
tain-world of peaks and pines. I put on my snowshoes, climbed upward beneath the moon, and
from the summit of Lead Mountain, thirteen
thousand feet high, saw the sun rise in splendor
on a world of white.

The tracks and records in the snow which I
read in passing made something of a daily newspaper for me. They told much of news of the
wilds. Sometimes I read of the games that the
snowshoe rabbit had played; of a starving time
among the brave mountain sheep on the heights;
of the quiet content in the ptarmigan neighborhood; of the dinner that the pines had given the
grouse; of the amusements and exercises on the
deer's stamping-ground; of the cunning of foxes;
of the visits of magpies, the excursions of lynxes,
and the red records of mountain lions.

The mountain lion is something of a game-
hog and an epicure. He prefers warm blood for
every meal, and is very wasteful. I have much

evidence against him; his worst one-day record that I have shows five tragedies. In this time he killed a mountain sheep, a fawn, a grouse, a rabbit, and a porcupine; and as if this were not enough, he was about to kill another sheep when a dark object on snowshoes shot down the slope near by and disturbed him. The instances where he has attacked human beings are rare, but he will watch and follow one for hours with the utmost caution and curiosity. One morning after a night-journey through the wood, I turned back and doubled my trail. After going a short distance I came to the track of a lion alongside my own. I went back several miles and read the lion's movements. He had watched me closely. At every place where I rested he had crept up close, and at the place where I had sat down against a stump he had crept up to the opposite side of the stump, — and I fear while I dozed!

One night during this expedition I had lodging in an old and isolated prospector's cabin, with two young men who had very long hair. For months they had been in seclusion, "gathering wonderful herbs," hunting out prescriptions for every human ill, and waiting for their hair to grow long. I hope they prepared some helpful, or at least harmless prescriptions, for, ere this, they have become picturesque, and I fear prosperous, medicine-men on some populous street-corner. One day I had dinner on the summit of Mt. Lincoln, fourteen thousand feet above the ocean. I ate with some miners who were digging out their fortune; and was " the only caller in five months."

But I was not always a welcome guest. At one of the big mining-camps I stopped for mail and to rest for a day or so. I was all " rags and tags," and had several broken strata of geology and charcoal on my face in addition. Before I had got well into the town, from all quarters came dogs, each of which seemed determined to make it necessary for me to buy some clothes. As I had already determined to do this, I kept the dogs at bay for a time, and then sought refuge in a first-class hotel; from this the porter, stimulated by an excited order from the clerk, promptly and literally kicked me out!

In the robings of winter how different the

mountains than when dressed in the bloom of
summer! In no place did the change seem more
marked than on some terrace over which summer flung the lacy drapery of a white cascade,
or where a wild waterfall "leapt in glory."
These places in winter were glorified with the
fine arts of ice, — "frozen music," as some one
has defined architecture, — for here winter had
constructed from water a wondrous array of
columns, panels, filigree, fretwork, relief-work,
arches, giant icicles, and stalagmites as large as,
and in ways resembling, a big tree with a fluted
full-length mantle of ice.

Along the way were extensive areas covered
with the ruins of fire-killed trees. Most of the
forest fires which had caused these were the result of carelessness. The timber destroyed by
these fires had been needed by thousands of
home-builders. The robes of beauty which they
had burned from the mountain-sides are a serious loss. These fire ruins preyed upon me, and I
resolved to do something to save the remaining
forests. The opportunity came shortly after the
resolution was made.

Colorado Snow Observer

Two days before reaching the objective point, farthest south, my food gave out, and I fasted. But as soon as I reached the end, I started to descend the heights, and very naturally knocked at the door of the first house I came to, and asked for something to eat. I supposed I was at a pioneer's cabin. A handsome, neatly dressed young lady came to the door, and when her eyes fell upon me she blushed and then turned pale. I was sorry that my appearance had alarmed her, but I repeated my request for something to eat. Just then, through the half-open door behind the young lady, came the laughter of children, and a glance into the room told me that I was before a mountain schoolhouse. By this time the teacher, to whom I was talking, startled me by inviting me in. As I sat eating a luncheon to which the teacher and each one of the six school-children contributed, the teacher explained to me that she was recently from the East, and that I so well fitted her ideas of a Western desperado that she was frightened at first. When I finished eating, I made my first after-dinner speech; it was also my first attempt to make a forestry address. One point I tried to bring out was concerning the destruction wrought by forest fires. Among other things I said: "During the past few years in Colorado, forest fires, which ought never to have been started, have destroyed many million dollars' worth of timber, and the area over which the fires have burned aggregates twenty-five thousand square miles. This area of forest would put on the equator an evergreen-forest belt one mile wide that would reach entirely around the world. Along with this forest have perished many of the animals and thousands of beautiful birds who had homes in it."

I finally bade all good-bye, went on my way rejoicing, and in due course arrived at Denver, where a record of one of my longest winter excursions was written.

In order to give an idea of one of my briefer winter walks, I close this chapter with an account of a round-trip snowshoe journey from Estes Park to Grand Lake, the most thrilling and adventurous that has ever entertained me on the trail.

One February morning I set off alone on snowshoes to cross the "range," for the purpose

of making some snow-measurements. The nature
of my work for the State required the closest observation of the character and extent of the snow
in the mountains. I hoped to get to Grand Lake
for the night, but I was on the east side of the
range, and Grand Lake was on the west. Along
the twenty-five miles of trail there was only wilderness, without a single house. The trail was
steep and the snow very soft. Five hours were
spent in gaining timber-line, which was only six
miles from my starting-place, but four thousand
feet above it. Rising in bold grandeur above me
was the summit of Long's Peak, and this, with
the great hills of drifted snow, out of which here
and there a dwarfed and distorted tree thrust its
top, made timber-line seem weird and lonely.

From this point the trail wound for six miles
across bleak heights before it came down to timber on the other side of the range. I set forward
as rapidly as possible, for the northern sky looked
stormy. I must not only climb up fifteen hundred feet, but must also skirt the icy edges of
several precipices in order to gain the summit.
My friends had warned me that the trip was a

foolhardy one even on a clear, calm day, but I was fated to receive the fury of a snowstorm while on the most broken portion of the trail.

The tempest came on with deadly cold and almost blinding violence. The wind came with awful surges, and roared and boomed among the crags. The clouds dashed and seethed along the surface, shutting out all landmarks. I was every moment in fear of slipping or being blown over a precipice, but there was no shelter; I was on the roof of the continent, twelve thousand five hundred feet above sea-level, and to stop in the bitter cold meant death.

It was still three miles to timber on the west slope, and I found it impossible to keep the trail. Fearing to perish if I tried to follow even the general course of the trail, I abandoned it altogether, and started for the head of a gorge, down which I thought it would be possible to climb to the nearest timber. Nothing definite could be seen. The clouds on the snowy surface and the light electrified air gave the eye only optical illusions. The outline of every object was topsy-turvy and dim. The large stones that I thought to step

THE CREST OF THE CONTINENT IN WINTER, 13,000 FEET ABOVE SEA-LEVEL

on were not there; and, when apparently passing others, I bumped into them. Several times I fell headlong by stepping out for a drift and finding a depression.

In the midst of these illusions I walked out on a snow-cornice that overhung a precipice! Unable to see clearly, I had no realization of my danger until I felt the snow giving way beneath me. I had seen the precipice in summer, and knew it was more than a thousand feet to the bottom! Down I tumbled, carrying a large fragment of the snow-cornice with me. I could see nothing, and I was entirely helpless. Then, just as the full comprehension of the awful thing that was happening swept over me, the snow falling beneath me suddenly stopped. I plunged into it, completely burying myself. Then I, too, no longer moved downward; my mind gradually admitted the knowledge that my body, together with a considerable mass of the snow, had fallen upon a narrow ledge and caught there. More of the snow came tumbling after me, and it was a matter of some minutes before I succeeded in extricating myself.

When I thrust my head out of the snow-mass and looked about me, I was first appalled by a glance outward, which revealed the terrible height of the precipice on the face of which I was hanging. Then I was relieved by a glance upward, which showed me that I was only some twenty feet from the top, and that a return thither would not be very difficult. But if I had walked from the top a few feet farther back, I should have fallen a quarter of a mile.

One of my snowshoes came off as I struggled out, so I took off the other shoe and used it as a scoop to uncover the lost web. But it proved very slow and dangerous work. With both shoes off I sank chest-deep in the snow; if I ventured too near the edge of the ledge, the snow would probably slip off and carry me to the bottom of the precipice. It was only after two hours of effort that the shoe was recovered.

When I first struggled to the surface of the snow on the ledge, I looked at once to find a way back to the top of the precipice. I quickly saw that by following the ledge a few yards beneath the unbroken snow-cornice I could climb to the

18

top over some jagged rocks. As soon as I had recovered the shoe, I started round the ledge. When I had almost reached the jagged rocks, the snow-cornice caved upon me, and not only buried me, but came perilously near knocking me into the depths beneath. But at last I stood upon the top in safety.

A short walk from the top brought me out upon a high hill of snow that sloped steeply down into the woods. The snow was soft, and I sat down in it and slid "a blue streak"—my blue overalls recording the streak — for a quarter of a mile, and then came to a sudden and confusing stop; one of my webs had caught on a spine of one of the dwarfed and almost buried trees at timber-line.

When I had traveled a short distance below timber-line, a fearful crashing caused me to turn; I was in time to see fragments of snow flying in all directions, and snow-dust boiling up in a great geyser column. A snow-slide had swept down and struck a granite cliff. As I stood there, another slide started on the heights above timber, and with a far-off roar swept down in awful mag-

nificence, with a comet-like tail of snow-dust.
Just at timber-line it struck a ledge and glanced
to one side, and at the same time shot up into
the air so high that for an instant I saw the
treetops beneath it. But it came back to earth
with awful force, and I felt the ground trem-
ble as it crushed a wide way through the woods.
It finally brought up at the bottom of a gulch
with a wreckage of hundreds of noble spruce
trees that it had crushed down and swept before it.

As I had left the trail on the heights, I was
now far from it and in a rugged and wholly un-
frequented section, so that coming upon the fresh
tracks of a mountain lion did not surprise me.
But I was not prepared for what occurred soon
afterward. Noticing a steamy vapor rising from
a hole in the snow by the protruding roots of an
overturned tree, I walked to the hole to learn the
cause of it. One whiff of the vapor stiffened my
hair and limbered my legs. I shot down a steep
slope, dodging trees and rocks. The vapor was
rank with the odor from a bear.

At the bottom of the slope I found the frozen

A SNOW-SLIDE TRACK

surface of a stream much easier walking than the soft snow. All went well until I came to some rapids, where, with no warning whatever, the thin ice dropped me into the cold current among the boulders. I scrambled to my feet, with the ice flying like broken glass. The water came only a little above my knees, but as I had gone under the surface, and was completely drenched, I made an enthusiastic move toward the bank. Now snowshoes are not adapted for walking either in swift water or among boulders. I realized this thoroughly after they had several times tripped me, sprawling, into the liquid cold. Finally I sat down in the water, took them off, and came out gracefully.

I gained the bank with chattering teeth and an icy armor. My pocket thermometer showed two degrees above zero. Another storm was bearing down upon me from the range, and the sun was sinking. But the worst of it all was that there were several miles of rough and strange country between me and Grand Lake that would have to be made in the dark. I did not care to take any more chances on the ice, so I spent a hard hour climbing out of the cañon. The climb warmed me and set my clothes steaming.

My watch indicated six o'clock. A fine snow was falling, and it was dark and cold. I had been exercising for twelve hours without rest, and had eaten nothing since the previous day, as I never take breakfast. I made a fire and lay down on a rock by it to relax, and also to dry my clothes. In half an hour I started on again. Rocky and forest-covered ridges lay between me and Grand Lake. In the darkness I certainly took the worst way. I met with too much resistance in the thickets and too little on the slippery places, so that when, at eleven o'clock that night, I entered a Grand Lake Hotel, my appearance was not prepossessing.

The next day, after a few snow-measurements, I set off to re-cross the range. In order to avoid warm bear-dens and cold streams, I took a different route. It was a much longer way than the one I had come by, so I went to a hunter's deserted cabin for the night. The cabin had no door, and I could see the stars through the roof. The old sheet-iron stove was badly rusted and broken. Most of the night I spent chopping wood, and I did not sleep at all. But I had a good rest by the stove, where I read a little from a musty pamphlet on palmistry that I found between the logs of the cabin. I always carry candles with me. When the wind is blowing, the wood damp, and the fingers numb, they are of inestimable value in kindling a fire. I do not carry firearms, and during the night, when a lion gave a blood-freezing screech, I wished he were somewhere else.

Daylight found me climbing toward the top of the range through the Medicine Bow National Forest, among some of the noblest evergreens in Colorado. When the sun came over the range, the silent forest vistas became magnificent with bright lights and deep shadows. At timber-line the bald rounded summit of the range, like a gigantic white turtle, rose a thousand feet above me. The slope was steep and very icy; a gusty wind whirled me about. Climbing to the top would be like going up a steep ice-covered house-roof. It would be a dangerous and barely possible undertaking. But as I did not have courage enough to retreat, I threw off my snowshoes and started up. I cut a place in the ice for every step. There was nothing to hold to, and a slip meant a fatal slide.

With rushes from every quarter, the wind did its best to freeze or overturn me. My ears froze, and my fingers grew so cold that they could hardly hold the ice-axe. But after an hour of constant peril and ever-increasing exhaustion, I got above the last ice and stood upon the snow. The snow was solidly packed, and, leaving my snowshoes strapped across my shoulders, I went scrambling up. Near the top of the range a ledge of granite cropped out through the snow, and toward this I hurried. Before making a final spurt to the ledge, I paused to breathe. As I stopped, I was startled by sounds like the creaking of wheels on a cold, snowy street. The snow beneath me was slipping! I had started a snowslide.

Almost instantly the slide started down the slope with me on it. The direction in which it was going and the speed it was making would in a few seconds carry it down two thousand feet of

slope, where it would leap over a precipice into
the woods. I was on the very upper edge of the
snow that had started, and this was the tail-end
of the slide. I tried to stand up in the rushing
snow, but its speed knocked my feet from under
me, and in an instant I was rolled beneath the
surface. Beneath the snow, I went tumbling on
with it for what seemed like a long time, but I
know, of course, that it was for only a second or
two; then my feet struck against something solid.
I was instantly flung to the surface again, where
I either was spilled off, or else fell through, the
end of the slide, and came to a stop on the
scraped and frozen ground, out of the grasp of
the terrible snow.

I leaped to my feet and saw the slide sweep on
in most impressive magnificence. At the front
end of the slide the snow piled higher and higher,
while following in its wake were splendid stream-
ers and scrolls of snow-dust. I lost no time in
getting to the top, and set off southward, where,
after six miles, I should come to the trail that led
to my starting-place on the east side of the range.
After I had made about three miles, the cold

clouds closed in, and everything was fogged. A chilly half-hour's wait and the clouds broke up. I had lost my ten-foot staff in the snow-slide, and feeling for precipices without it would probably bring me out upon another snow-cornice, so I took no chances.

I was twelve thousand five hundred feet above sea-level when the clouds broke up, and from this great height I looked down upon what seemed to be the margin of the polar world. It was intensely cold, but the sun shone with dazzling glare, and the wilderness of snowy peaks came out like a grand and jagged ice-field in the far south. Halos and peculiarly luminous balls floated through the color-tinged and electrical air. The horizon had a touch of cobalt blue, and on the dome above, white flushes appeared and disappeared like faint auroras. After five hours on these silent but imposing heights I struck my first day's trail, and began a wild and merry coast down among the rocks and trees to my starting-place.

I hope to have more winter excursions, but perhaps I have had my share. At the bare thought of those winter experiences I am again on an unsheltered peak struggling in a storm; or I am in a calm and spendid forest upon whose snowy, peaceful aisles fall the purple shadows of crags and pines.

The Story of a Thousand-Year Pine

The Story of a Thousand-Year Pine

THE peculiar charm and fascination that trees exert over many people I had always felt from childhood, but it was that great nature-lover, John Muir, who first showed me how and where to learn their language. Few trees, however, ever held for me such an attraction as did a gigantic and venerable yellow pine which I discovered one autumn day several years ago while exploring the southern Rockies. It grew within sight of the Cliff-Dwellers' Mesa Verde, which stands at the corner of four States, and as I came upon it one evening just as the sun was setting over that mysterious tableland, its character and heroic proportions made an impression upon me that I shall never forget, and which familiar acquaintance only served to deepen while it yet lived and before the axeman came. Many a time I returned to build my camp-fire by it and have

31

a day or a night in its solitary and noble company. I learned afterwards that it had been given the name "Old Pine," and it certainly had an impressiveness quite compatible with the age and dignity which go with a thousand years of life.

When, one day, the sawmill-man at Mancos wrote, "Come, we are about to log your old pine," I started at once, regretting that a thing which seemed to me so human, as well as so noble, must be killed.

I went out with the axemen who were to cut the old pine down. A grand and impressive tree he was. Never have I seen so much individuality, so much character, in a tree. Although lightning had given him a bald crown, he was still a healthy giant, and was waving evergreen banners more than one hundred and fifteen feet above the earth. His massive trunk, eight feet in diameter on a level with my breast, was covered with a thick, rough, golden-brown bark which was broken into irregular plates. Several of his arms were bent and broken. Altogether, he presented a time-worn but heroic appearance.

A VETERAN WESTERN YELLOW PINE

Story of a Thousand-Year Pine

It is almost a marvel that trees should live to become the oldest of living things. Fastened in one place, their struggle is incessant and severe. From the moment a baby tree is born — from the instant it casts its tiny shadow upon the ground — until death, it is in danger from insects and animals. It cannot move to avoid danger. It cannot run away to escape enemies. Fixed in one spot, almost helpless, it must endure flood and drought, fire and storm, insects and earthquakes, or die.

Trees, like people, struggle for existence, and an aged tree, like an aged person, has not only a striking appearance, but an interesting biography. I have read the autobiographies of many century-old trees, and have found their life-stories strange and impressive. The yearly growth, or annual ring of wood with which trees envelop themselves, is embossed with so many of their experiences that this annual ring of growth literally forms an autobiographic diary of the tree's life.

I wanted to read Old Pine's autobiography. A veteran pine that had stood on the southern Rockies and struggled and triumphed through the changing seasons of hundreds of years must contain a rare life-story. From his stand between the Mesa and the pine-plumed mountain, he had seen the panorama of the seasons and many a strange pageant; he had beheld what scenes of animal and human strife, what storms and convulsions of nature! Many a wondrous secret he had locked within his tree soul. Yet, although he had not recorded what he had *seen*, I knew that he had kept a fairly accurate diary of his own personal experience. This I knew the saw would reveal, and this I had determined to see.

Nature matures a million conifer seeds for each one she chooses for growth, so we can only speculate as to the selection of the seed from which sprung this storied pine. It may be that the cone in which it matured was crushed into the earth by the hoof of a passing deer. It may have been hidden by a jay; or, as is more likely, it may have grown from one of the uneaten cones which a Douglas squirrel had buried for winter food. Douglas squirrels are the principal nurserymen for all the Western pineries. Each autumn they harvest a heavy percentage of the

cone crop and bury it for winter. The seeds in
the uneaten cones germinate, and each year countless thousands of conifers grow from the seeds
planted by these squirrels. It may be that the
seed from which Old Pine burst had been planted
by an ancient ancestor of the protesting Douglas
who was in possession, or this seed may have been
in a cone which simply bounded or blew into a
hole, where the seed found sufficient mould and
moisture to give it a start in life.

Two loggers swung their axes. At the first
blow a Douglas squirrel came out of a hole at
the base of a dead limb near the top of the tree
and made an aggressive claim of ownership, setting up a vociferous protest against the cutting.
As his voice was unheeded, he came scolding
down the tree, jumped off one of the lower limbs,
and took refuge in a young pine that stood near
by. From time to time he came out on the top
of the limb nearest to us, and, with a wry face,
fierce whiskers, and violent gestures, directed a
torrent of abuse at the axemen who were delivering death-blows to Old Pine.

Wild Life on the Rockies

The old pine's enormous weight caused him to fall heavily, and he came to earth with tremendous force and struck on an elbow of one of his stocky arms. The force of the fall not only broke the trunk in two, but badly shattered it. The damage to the log was so general that the sawmill-man said it would not pay to saw it into lumber and that it could rot on the spot.

I had come a long distance for the express purpose of deciphering Old Pine's diary as the scroll of his life should be laid open in the sawmill. The abandonment of the shattered form compelled the adoption of another way of getting at his story. Receiving permission to do as I pleased with his remains, I at once began to cut and split both the trunk and the limbs and to transcribe their strange records. Day after day I worked. I dug up the roots and thoroughly dissected them, and with the aid of a magnifier I studied the trunk, the roots, and the limbs.

I carefully examined the base of his stump, and in it I found 1047 rings of growth! He had lived through a thousand and forty-seven memorable years. As he was cut down in 1903, his birth probably occurred in 856.

In looking over the rings of growth, I found that a few of them were much thicker than the others; and these thick rings, or coats of wood, tell of favorable seasons. There were also a few extremely thin rings of growth. In places two and even three of these were together. These were the result of unfavorable seasons, — of drought or cold. The rings of trees also show healed wounds, and tell of burns, bites, and bruises, of torn bark and broken arms. Old Pine not only received injuries in his early years, but from time to time throughout his life. The somewhat kinked condition of several of the rings of growth, beginning with the twentieth, shows that at the age of twenty he sustained an injury which resulted in a severe curvature of the spine, and that for some years he was somewhat stooped. I was unable to make out from his diary whether this injury was the result of a tree or some object falling upon him and pinning him down, or whether his back had been overweighted and bent by wet, clinging snow. As I could not find any scars or bruises, I think that snow must have been the cause of the injury. However, after a few years he straightened up with youthful vitality and seemed to outgrow and forget the experience.

A century of tranquil life followed, and during these years the rapid growth tells of good seasons as well as good soil. This rapid growth also shows that there could not have been any crowding neighbors to share the sun and the soil. The tree had grown evenly in all quarters, and the pith of the tree was in the centre. But had one tree grown close, on that quarter the old pine would have grown slower than the others and would have been thinner, and the pith would thus have been away from the tree's centre.

When the old pine was just completing his one hundred and thirty-fifth ring of growth, he met with an accident which I can account for only by assuming that a large tree that grew several yards away blew over, and in falling, stabbed him in the side with two dead limbs. His bark was broken and torn, but this healed in due time. Short sections of the dead limbs broke off, however, and were embedded in the old pine. Twelve years' growth covered them, and they remained hidden from view until my splitting revealed them. The other wounds started promptly to heal and, with one exception, did so.

A year or two later some ants and borers began excavating their deadly winding ways in the old pine. They probably started to work in one of the places injured by the falling tree. They must have had some advantage, or else something must have happened to the nuthatches and chickadees that year, for, despite the vigilance of these birds, both the borers and the ants succeeded in establishing colonies that threatened injury and possibly death.

Fortunately relief came. One day the chief surgeon of all the Southwestern pineries came along. This surgeon was the Texas woodpecker. He probably did not long explore the ridges and little furrows of the bark before he discovered the wound or heard these hidden insects working. After a brief examination, holding his ear to the bark for a moment to get the location of the tree's deadly foe beneath, he was ready to act.

He made two successful operations. These not only required him to cut deeply into the old pine and take out the borers, but he may also have had to come back from time to time to dress the wounds by devouring the ant-colonies which may have persisted in taking possession of them. The wounds finally healed, and only the splitting of the affected parts revealed these records, all filled with pitch and preserved for nearly nine hundred years.

Following this, an even tenor marked his life for nearly three centuries. This quiet existence came to an end in the summer of 1301, when a stroke of lightning tore a limb out of his round top and badly shattered a shoulder. He had barely recovered from this injury when a violent wind tore off several of his arms. During the summer of 1348 he lost two of his largest arms. These were large and sound, and were more than a foot in diameter at the points of breakage. As these were broken by a down-pressing weight or force, we may attribute these breaks to accumulations of snow.

The oldest, largest portion of a tree is the short

section immediately above the ground, and, as this lower section is the most exposed to accidents or to injuries from enemies, it generally bears evidence of having suffered the most. Within its scroll are usually found the most extensive and interesting autobiographical impressions.

It is doubtful if there is any portion of the earth upon which there are so many deadly struggles as upon the earth around the trunk of a tree. Upon this small arena there are battles fierce and wild; here nature is "red in tooth and claw." When a tree is small and tender, countless insects come to feed upon it. Birds come to it to devour these insects. Around the tree are daily almost merciless fights for existence. These death-struggles occur not only in the daytime, but in the night. Mice, rats, and rabbits destroy millions of young trees. These bold animals often flay baby trees in the daylight, and while at their deadly feast many a time have they been surprised by hawks, and then they are at a banquet where they themselves are eaten. The owl, the faithful nightwatchman of trees, often swoops down at night, and as a result some little tree is splashed with the blood of the very animal that came to feed upon it.

The lower section of Old Pine's trunk contained records which I found interesting. One of these in particular aroused my imagination. I was sawing off a section of this lower portion when the saw, with a buzz-z-z-z, suddenly jumped. The object struck was harder than the saw. I wondered what it could be, and, cutting the wood carefully away, laid bare a flint arrowhead. Close to this one I found another, and then with care I counted the rings of growth to find out the year that these had wounded Old Pine. The outer ring which these arrowheads had pierced was the six hundred and thirtieth, so that the year of this occurrence was 1486.

Had an Indian bent his bow and shot at a bear that had stood at bay backed up against this tree? Or was there around this tree a battle among Indian tribes? Is it possible that at this place some Cliff-Dweller scouts encountered their advancing foe from the north and opened hostilities? It may be that around Old Pine was fought the battle that is said to have decided the fate of that mysterious race the Cliff-Dwellers. The imagination insists on speculating with these two arrowheads, though they form a fascinating clue that leads us to no definite conclusion. But the fact remains that Old Pine was wounded by two Indian arrowheads some time during his six hundred and thirtieth summer.

The year that Columbus discovered America, Old Pine was a handsome giant with a round head held more than one hundred feet above the earth. He was six hundred and thirty-six years old, and with the coming of the Spanish adventurers his lower trunk was given new events to record. The year 1540 was a particularly memorable one for him. This year brought the first horses and bearded men into the drama which was played around him. This year, for the first time, he felt the edge of steel and the tortures of fire. The old chronicles say that the Spanish explorers found the cliff-houses in the year 1540. I believe that during this year a Spanish exploring party may have camped beneath Old Pine and built a fire against his instep, and that some of the explorers hacked him with an axe. The old pine had distinct records of axe and fire markings during the year 1540. It was not common for the Indians of the West to burn or mutilate trees, and as it was common for the Spaniards to do so, and as these hackings in the tree seemed to have been made with some edged tool sharper than any possessed by the Indians, it at least seems probable that they were done by the Spaniards. At any rate, from the year 1540 until the day of his death, Old Pine carried these scars on his instep.

As the average yearly growth of the old pine was about the same as in trees similarly situated at the present time, I suppose that climatic conditions in his early days must have been similar to the climatic conditions of to-day. His records indicate periods of even tenor of climate, a year of extremely poor conditions, occasionally a year crowned with a bountiful wood harvest. From 1540 to 1762 I found little of special interest. In 1762, however, the season was not regular. After the ring was well started, something, perhaps a cold wave, for a time checked its growth, and as a result the wood for that one year resembled two years' growth, but yet the difference between this double or false ring and a regular one was easily detected. Old Pine's " hard times " experience seems to have been during the years 1804 and 1805. I think it probable that these were years of drought. During 1804 the layer of wood was the thinnest in his life, and for 1805 the only wood I could find was a layer which only partly covered the trunk of the tree, and this was exceedingly thin.

From time to time in the old pine's record, I came across what seemed to be indications of an earthquake shock; but late in 1811 or early in 1812, I think there is no doubt that he experienced a violent shock, for he made extensive records of it. This earthquake occurred after the sap had ceased to flow in 1811, and before it began to flow in the spring of 1812. In places the wood was checked and shattered. At one point, some distance from the ground, there was a bad horizontal break. Two big roots were broken in two, and that quarter of the tree which faced the cliffs had suffered from a rock bombardment. I suppose the violence of the quake displaced many rocks, and some of these, as they came bounding down the mountain-side, collided with Old Pine. One, of about five pounds' weight, struck him so violently in the side that it remained embedded there. After some years the wound was healed over, but this fragment remained in the tree until I released it.

During 1859 some one made an axe-mark on the old pine that may have been intended for a trail-blaze, and during the same year another fire badly burned and scarred his ankle. I wonder if some prospectors came this way in 1859 and made camp by him.

Another record of man's visits to the tree was made in the summer of 1881, when I think a hunting or outing party may have camped near here and amused themselves by shooting at a mark on Old Pine's ankle. Several modern rifle-bullets were found embedded in the wood around or just beneath a blaze which was made on the tree the same year in which the bullets had entered it. As both these marks were made during the year 1881, it is at least possible that

this year the old pine was used as the background for a target during a shooting contest.

While I was working over the old pine, a
Douglas squirrel who lived near by used every
day to stop in his busy harvesting of pine-cones
to look on and scold me. As I watched him
placing his cones in a hole in the ground under
the pine-needles, I often wondered if one of his
buried cones would remain there uneaten to
germinate and expand ever green into the air,
and become a noble giant to live as long and
as useful a life as Old Pine. I found myself
trying to picture the scenes in which this tree
would stand when the birds came singing back
from the Southland in the springtime of the year
3000.

After I had finished my work of splitting,
studying, and deciphering the fragments of the
old pine, I went to the sawmill and arranged for
the men to come over that evening after I had
departed and burn every piece and vestige of the
venerable old tree. I told them I should be gone
by dark. Then I went back and piled into a
pyramid every fragment of root and trunk and

broken branch. Seating myself upon this pyramid, I spent some time that afternoon gazing
through the autumn sunglow at the hazy Mesa
Verde, while my mind rebuilt and shifted the
scenes of the long, long drama in which Old
Pine had played his part, and of which he had
given us but a few fragmentary records. I lingered there dreaming until twilight. I thought
of the cycles during which he had stood patient in his appointed place, and my imagination busied itself with the countless experiences
that had been recorded, and the scenes and
pageants he had witnessed but of which he had
made no record. I wondered if he had enjoyed
the changing of seasons. I knew that he had
often boomed or hymned in the storm or in the
breeze. Many a monumental robe of snow-flowers
had he worn. More than a thousand times he
had beheld the earth burst into bloom amid the
happy songs of mating birds; hundreds of times
in summer he had worn countless crystal rain-
jewels in the sunlight of the breaking storm,
while the brilliant rainbow came and vanished on
the near-by mountain-side. Ten thousand times

he had stood silent in the lonely light of the white and mystic moon.

Twilight was fading into darkness when I arose and started on a night-journey for the Mesa Verde, where I intended next morning to greet an old gnarled cedar which grew on its summit. When I arrived at the top of the Mesa, I looked back and saw a pyramid of golden flame standing out in the darkness.

The Beaver and his Works

The Beaver and his Works

J HAVE never been able to decide which I love best, birds or trees, but as these are really comrades it does not matter, for they can take first place together. But when it comes to second place in my affection for wild things, this, I am sure, is filled by the beaver. The beaver has so many interesting ways, and is altogether so useful, so thrifty, so busy, so skillful, and so picturesque, that I believe his life and his deeds deserve a larger place in literature and a better place in our hearts. His engineering works are of great value to man. They not only help to distribute the waters and beneficially control the flow of the streams, but they also catch and save from loss enormous quantities of the earth's best plant-food. In helping to do these two things, — governing the rivers and fixing the soil, — he plays an important part, and if he and the forest had their way with the water-supply, floods would be prevented, streams would never run dry, and a comparatively even flow of water would be maintained in the rivers every day of the year.

A number of beaver establishing a colony made one of the most interesting exhibitions of constructive work that I have ever watched. The work went on for several weeks, and I spent hours and days in observing operations. My hiding-place on a granite crag allowed me a good view of the work, — the cutting and transportation of the little logs, the dam-building, and the house-raising. I was close to the trees that were felled. Occasionally, during the construction work of this colony, I saw several beaver at one time cutting trees near one another. Upon one occasion, one was squatted on a fallen tree, another on the limb of a live one, and a third upon a boulder, each busy cutting down his tree. In every case, the tail was used for a combination stool and brace. While cutting, the beaver sat upright and clasped the willow with fore paws or put his hands against the tree, usually tilting his head to one side. The average diameter of the trees cut was about four inches, and a tree of this size was cut down quickly and without a pause.

The Beaver and His Works

When the tree was almost cut off, the cutter usually thumped with his tail, at which signal all other cutters near by scampered away. But this warning signal was not always given, and in one instance an unwarned cutter had a narrow escape from a tree falling perilously close to him.

Before cutting a tree, a beaver usually paused and appeared to look at its surroundings as if choosing a place to squat or sit while cutting it down; but so far as I could tell, he gave no thought as to the direction in which the tree was going to fall. This is true of every beaver which I have seen begin cutting, and I have seen scores. But beavers have individuality, and occasionally I noticed one with marked skill or decision. It may be, therefore, that some beaver try to fell trees on a particular place. In fact, I remember having seen in two localities stumps which suggested that the beaver who cut down the trees had planned just how they were to fall. In the first locality, I could judge only from the record left by the stumps; but the quarter on which the main notch had been made, together with the fact that the notch had in two instances been made on a quarter of the tree where it was inconvenient for the cutter to work, seemed to indicate a plan to fell the tree in a particular direction. In the other locality, I knew the attitude of the trees before they were cut, and in this instance the evidence was so complete and conclusive that I must believe the beaver that cut down these trees endeavored to get them to fall in a definite direction. In each of these cases, however, judging chiefly from the teeth-marks, I think the cuttings were done by the same beaver. Many observations induce me to believe, however, that the majority of beaver do not plan how the trees are to fall.

Once a large tree is on the ground, the limbs are trimmed off and the trunk is cut into sections sufficiently small to be dragged, rolled, or pushed to the water, where transportation is easy.

The young beaver that I have seen cutting trees have worked in leisurely manner, in contrast with the work of the old ones. After giving a few bites, they usually stop to eat a piece of the bark, or to stare listlessly around for a time. As workers, young beaver appear at their best and liveliest when taking a limb from the hillside to the house in the pond. A young beaver will catch a limb by one end in his teeth, and, throwing it over his shoulder in the attitude of a puppy racing with a rope or a rag, make off to the pond. Once in the water, he throws up his head and swims to the house or the dam with the limb held trailing out over his back.

The typical beaver-house seen in the Rockies at the present time stands in the upper edge of the pond which the beaver-dam has made, near where the brook enters it. Its foundation is about eight feet across, and it stands from five to ten feet in height, a rude cone in form. Most houses are made of sticks and mud, and are apparently put up with little thought for the living-room, which is later dug or gnawed from the interior. The entrance to the house is below water-level, and commonly on the bottom of the lake. Late each autumn, the house is plastered on the outside with mud, and I am inclined to believe that this plaster is not so much to increase the warmth of the house as to give it, when the mud is frozen, a strong protective armor, an armor which will prevent the winter enemies of the beaver from breaking into the house.

Each autumn beaver pile up near by the house, a large brush-heap of green trunks and limbs, mostly of aspen, willow, cottonwood, or alder. This is their granary, and during the winter they feed upon the green bark, supplementing this with the roots of water-plants, which they drag from the bottom of the pond.

Along in May five baby beaver appear, and a little later these explore the pond and race, wrestle, and splash water in it as merrily as boys. Occasionally they sun themselves on a fallen log, or play together there, trying to push one another off into the water. Often they play in the canals that lead between ponds or from them, or on the "slides." Toward the close of summer, they have their lessons in cutting and dam-building.

A beaver appears awkward as he works on land. In use of arms and hands he reminds one of a monkey, while his clumsy and usually slow-moving body will often suggest the hippopotamus. By using head, hands, teeth, tail, and

A BEAVER-HOUSE

Supply of winter food piled on the right

The Beaver and His Works

webbed feet the beaver accomplishes much. The tail of a beaver is a useful and much-used appendage; it serves as a rudder, a stool, and a ramming or signal club. The beaver *may* use his tail for a trowel, but I have never seen him so use it. His four front teeth are excellent edge-tools for his logging and woodwork; his webbed feet are most useful in his deep-waterway transportation, and his hands in house-building and especially in dam-building. It is in dam-building that the beaver shows his greatest skill and his best headwork; for I confess to the belief that a beaver reasons. I have so often seen him change his plans so wisely and meet emergencies so promptly and well that I can think of him only as a reasoner.

I have often wondered if beaver make a preliminary survey of a place before beginning to build a dam. I have seen them prowling suggestively along brooks just prior to beaver-dam building operations there, and circumstantial evidence would credit them with making preliminary surveys. But of this there is no proof. I have noticed a few things that seem to have been considered by beaver before beginning dam-building, — the supply of food and of dam-building material, for instance, and the location of the dam so as to require the minimum amount of material and insure the creation of the largest reservoir. In making the dam, the beaver usually takes advantage of boulders, willow-clumps, and surface irregularities. But he often makes errors of judgment. I have seen him abandon dams both before and after completion. The apparent reasons were that the dam either had failed or would fail to flood the area which he needed or desired flooded. His endeavors are not always successful. About twenty years ago, near Helena, Montana, a number of beaver made an audacious attempt to dam the Missouri River. After long and persistent effort, however, they gave it up. The beaver may be credited with errors, failures, and successes. He has forethought. If a colony of beaver be turned loose upon a three-mile tree-lined brook in the wilds and left undisturbed for a season, or until they have had time to select a site and locate themselves to best advantage, it is probable that the location chosen will indicate that they have examined the entire brook and then selected the best place.

As soon as the beaver's brush dam is completed, it begins to accumulate trash and mud. In a little while, usually, it is covered with a mass of soil, shrubs of willow begin to grow upon it, and after a few years it is a strong, earthy, willow-covered dam. The dams vary in length from a few feet to several hundred feet. I measured one on the South Platte River that was eleven hundred feet long.

The influence of a beaver-dam is astounding. As soon as completed, it becomes a highway for the folk of the wild. It is used day and night. Mice and porcupines, bears and rabbits, lions and wolves, make a bridge of it. From it, in the evening, the graceful deer cast their reflections in the quiet pond. Over it dash pursuer and pursued; and on it take place battles and courtships. It is often torn by hoof and claw of animals locked in death-struggles, and often, very often, it is stained with blood. Many a drama, picturesque, fierce, and wild, is staged upon a beaver-dam.

An interesting and valuable book could be

written concerning the earth as modified and benefited by beaver action, and I have long thought that the beaver deserved at least a chapter in Marsh's masterly book, "The Earth as modified by Human Action." To "work like a beaver" is an almost universal expression for energetic persistence, but who realizes that the beaver has accomplished anything? Almost unread of and unknown are his monumental works.

The instant a beaver-dam is completed, it has a decided influence on the flow of the water, and especially on the quantity of sediment which the passing water carries. The sediment, instead of going down to fill the channel below, or to clog the river's mouth, fill the harbor, and do damage a thousand miles away, is accumulated in the pond behind the dam, and a level deposit is formed over the entire area of the lake. By and by this deposit is so great that the lake is filled with sediment, but before this happens, both lake and dam check and delay so much flood-water that floods are diminished in volume, and the water thus delayed is in part added to the flow of the streams at the time of low water, the result being a more even stream-flow at all times.

The regulation of stream-flow is important. There are only a few rainy days each year, and all the water that flows down the rivers falls on these few rainy days. The instant the water reaches the earth, it is hurried away toward the sea, and unless some agency delays the run-off, the rivers would naturally contain water only on the rainy days and a little while after. The fact that some rivers contain water at all times is but evidence that something has held in check a portion of the water which fell during these rainy days.

Among the agencies which best perform this service of keeping the streams ever-flowing, are the forests and the works of the beaver. Rainfall accumulates in the brooks. The brooks conduct the water to the rivers. If across a river there be a beaver-dam, the pond formed by it will be a reservoir which will catch and retain some of the water coming into it during rainy days, and will thus delay the passage of all water which flows through it. Beaver-reservoirs are leaky ones, and if they are stored full during rainy days, the leaking helps to maintain the stream-flow in dry weather. A beaver-dam thus tends to distribute to the streams below it a moderate quantity of water each day. In other words, it spreads out or distributes the water of the few rainy days through all the days of the year. A river which flows steadily throughout the year is of inestimable value to mankind. If floods sweep a river, they do damage. If low water comes, the wheels of steamers and of manufactories cease to move, and damage or death may result. In maintaining a medium between the extremes of high and low water, the beaver's work is of profound importance. In helping beneficially to control a river, the beaver would render enormous service if allowed to construct his works at its source. During times of heavy rainfall, the water-flow carries with it, especially in unforested sections, great quantities of soil and sediment. Beaver-dams catch much of the material eroded from the hillsides above, and also prevent much erosion along the streams which they govern. They thus catch and deposit in place much valuable soil, the cream

A BEAVER-DAM IN WINTER

of the earth, that otherwise would be washed away and lost, — washed away into the rivers and harbors, impeding navigation and increasing river and harbor bills.

There is an old Indian legend which says that after the Creator separated the land from the water he employed gigantic beavers to smooth it down and prepare it for the abode of man. This is appreciative and suggestive. Beaver-dams have had much to do with the shaping and creating of a great deal of the richest agricultural land in America. To-day there are many peaceful and productive valleys the soil of which has been accumulated and fixed in place by ages of engineering activities on the part of the beaver before the white man came. On both mountain and plain you may still see much of this good work accomplished by them. In the mountains, deep and almost useless gulches have been filled by beaver-dams with sediment, and in course of time changed to meadows. So far as I know, the upper course of every river in the Rockies is through a number of beaver-meadows, some of them acres in extent.

Wild Life on the Rockies

On the upper course of Grand River in Colorado, I once made an extensive examination of some old beaver-works. Series of beaver-dams had been extended along this stream for several miles, as many as twenty dams to the mile. Each succeeding dam had backed water to the one above it. These had accumulated soil and formed a series of terraces, which, with the moderate slope of the valley, had in time formed an extensive and comparatively level meadow for a great distance along the river. The beaver settlement on this river was long ago almost entirely destroyed, and the year before my arrival a cloudburst had fallen upon the mountain-slope above, and the down-rushing flood had, in places, eroded deeply into the deposits formed by the beaver-works. At one place the water had cut down twenty-two feet, and had brought to light the fact that the deposit had been formed by a series of dams one above the other, a new dam having been built or the old one increased in height when the deposit of sediment had filled, or nearly filled, the pond. This is only one instance. There are thousands of similar places in the Rockies where beaver-dams have accumulated deposits of greater or less extent than those on the Grand River.

Only a few beaver remain, and though much of their work will endure to serve mankind, in many places their old work is gone or is going to ruin for the want of attention. We are paying dearly for the thoughtless and almost complete destruction of this animal. A live beaver is far more valuable to us than a dead one. Soil is eroding away, river-channels are filling, and most of the streams in the United States fluctuate between flood and low water. A beaver colony at the source of every stream would moderate these extremes and add to the picturesqueness and beauty of many scenes that are now growing ugly with erosion. We need to coöperate with the beaver. He would assist the work of reclamation, and be of great service in maintaining the deep-waterways. I trust he will be assisted in colonizing our National Forests, and allowed to cut timber there without a permit.

The beaver is the Abou-ben-Adhem of the wild. May his tribe increase.

The Wilds without Firearms

The Wilds without Firearms

AD I encountered the two gray wolves during my first unarmed camping-trip into the
wilds, the experience would hardly have suggested to me that going without firearms is the
best way to enjoy wild nature. But I had made
many unarmed excursions beyond the trail before I had that adventure, and the habit of going
without a gun was so firmly fixed and so satisfactory that even a perilous wolf encounter did
not arouse any desire for firearms. The habit
continued, and to-day the only way I can enjoy
the wilds is to leave guns behind.

On that autumn afternoon I was walking along
slowly, reflectively, in a deep forest. Not a breath
of air moved, and even the aspen's golden leaves
stood still in the sunlight. All was calm and
peaceful around and within me, when I came to
a little sunny frost-tanned grass-plot surrounded

by tall, crowding pines. I felt drawn to its warmth and repose and stepped joyfully into it. Suddenly two gray wolves sprang from almost beneath my feet and faced me defiantly. At a few feet distance they made an impressive show of ferocity, standing ready apparently to hurl themselves upon me.

Now the gray wolf is a powerful, savage beast, and directing his strong jaws, tireless muscles, keen scent, and all-seeing eyes are exceedingly nimble wits. He is well equipped to make the severe struggle for existence which his present environment compels. In many Western localities, despite the high price offered for his scalp, he has managed not only to live, but to increase and multiply. I had seen gray wolves pull down big game. On one occasion I had seen a vigorous long-horned steer fall after a desperate struggle with two of these fearfully fanged animals. Many times I had come across scattered bones which told of their triumph; and altogether I was so impressed with their deadliness that a glimpse of one of them usually gave me over to a temporary dread.

The Wilds without Firearms

The two wolves facing me seemed to have been asleep in the sun when I disturbed them. I realized the danger and was alarmed, of course, but my faculties were under control, were stimulated, indeed, to unusual alertness, and I kept a bold front and faced them without flinching. Their expression was one of mingled surprise and anger, together with the apparent determination to sell their lives as dearly as possible. I gave them all the attention which their appearance and their reputation demanded. Not once did I take my eyes off them. I held them at bay with my eyes. I still have a vivid picture of terribly gleaming teeth, bristling backs, and bulging muscles in savage readiness.

They made no move to attack. I was afraid to attack and I dared not run away. I remembered that some trees I could almost reach behind me had limbs that stretched out toward me, yet I felt that to wheel, spring for a limb, and swing up beyond their reach could not be done quickly enough to escape those fierce jaws.

Both sides were of the same mind, ready to fight, but not at all eager to do so. Under these conditions our nearness was embarrassing, and we faced each other for what seemed, to me at least, a long time. My mind working like lightning, I thought of several possible ways of escaping. I considered each at length, found it faulty, and dismissed it. Meanwhile, not a sound had been made. I had not moved, but something had to be done. Slowly I worked the small folding axe from its sheath, and with the slowest of movements placed it in my right coat-pocket with the handle up, ready for instant use. I did this with studied deliberation, lest a sudden movement should release the springs that held the wolves back. I kept on staring. Statues, almost, we must have appeared to the "camp-bird" whose call from a near-by limb told me we were observed, and whose nearness gave me courage. Then, looking the nearer of the two wolves squarely in the eye, I said to him, "Well, why don't you move?" as though we were playing checkers instead of the game of life. He made no reply, but the spell was broken. I believe that both sides had been bluffing. In attempting to use my kodak while continuing the bluff, I brought matters to a focus. "What a picture you fellows will make," I said aloud, as my right hand slowly worked the kodak out of the case which hung under my left arm. Still keeping up a steady fire of looks, I brought the kodak in front of me ready to focus, and then touched the spring that released the folding front. When the kodak mysteriously, suddenly opened before the wolves, they fled for their lives. In an instant they had cleared the grassy space and vanished into the woods. I did not get their picture.

With a gun, the wolf encounter could not have ended more happily. At any rate, I have not for a moment cared for a gun since I returned enthusiastic from my first delightful trip into the wilds without one. Out in the wilds with nature is one of the safest and most sanitary of places. Bears are not seeking to devour, and the death-list from lions, wolves, snakes, and all other bugbears combined does not equal the death-list from fire, automobiles, street-cars, or banquets. Being afraid of nature or a rainstorm is like being afraid of the dark.

The time of that first excursion was spent

among scenes that I had visited before, but the discoveries I made and the deeper feelings it stirred within me, led me to think it more worth while than any previous trip among the same delightful scenes. The first day, especially, was excitingly crowded with new sights and sounds and fancies. I fear that during the earlier trips the rifle had obscured most of the scenes in which it could not figure, and as a result I missed fairyland and most of the sunsets.

When I arrived at the alpine lake by which I was to camp, evening's long rays and shadows were romantically robing the picturesque wild border of the lake. The crags, the temples, the flower-edged snowdrifts, and the grass-plots of this wild garden seemed half-unreal, as over them the long lights and torn shadows grouped and changed, lingered and vanished, in the last moments of the sun. The deep purple of evening was over all, and the ruined crag with the broken pine on the ridge-top was black against the evening's golden glow, when I hastened to make camp by a pine temple while the beautiful world of sunset's hour slowly faded into the night.

LAKE ODESSA

The Wilds without Firearms

The camp-fire was a glory-burst in the darkness, and the small many-spired evergreen temple before me shone an illuminated cathedral in the night. All that evening I believed in fairies, and by watching the changing camp-fire kept my fancies frolicking in realms of mystery where all the world was young. I lay down without a gun, and while the fire changed and faded to black and gray the coyotes began to howl. But their voices did not seem as lonely or menacing as when I had had a rifle by my side. As I lay listening to them, I thought I detected merriment in their tones, and in a little while their shouts rang as merrily as though they were boys at play. Never before had I realized that coyotes too had enjoyments, and I listened to their shouts with pleasure. At last the illumination faded from the cathedral grove and its templed top stood in charcoal against the clear heavens as I fell asleep beneath the peaceful stars.

The next morning I loitered here and there, getting acquainted with the lake-shore, for without a gun all objects, or my eyes, were so changed that I had only a dim recollection of having seen the place before. From time to time, as I walked about, I stopped to try to win the confidence of the small folk in fur and feathers. I found some that trusted me, and at noon a chipmunk, a camp-bird, a chickadee, and myself were several times busy with the same bit of luncheon at once.

Some years ago mountain sheep often came in flocks to lick the salty soil in a ruined crater on Specimen Mountain. One day I climbed up and hid myself in the crags to watch them. More than a hundred of them came. After licking for a time, many lay down. Some of the rams posed themselves on the rocks in heroic attitudes and looked serenely and watchfully around. Young lambs ran about, and a few occasionally raced up and down smooth, rocky steeps, seemingly without the slightest regard for the laws of falling bodies. I was close to the flock, but luckily they did not suspect my presence. After enjoying their fine wild play for more than two hours, I slipped away and left them in their home among the crags.

One spring day I paused in a whirl of mist

78

and wet snow to look for the trail. I could see only a few yards ahead. As I peered ahead, a bear emerged from the gloom, heading straight for me. Behind her were two cubs. I caught her impatient expression when she beheld me. She stopped, and then, with a growl of anger, she wheeled and boxed cubs right and left like an angry mother. The bears disappeared in the direction from which they had come, the cubs urged on with spanks from behind as all vanished in the falling snow.

The gray Douglas squirrel is one of the most active, audacious, and outspoken of animals. He enjoys seclusion and claims to be monarch of all he surveys, and no trespasser is too big to escape a scolding from him. Many times he has given me a terrible tongue-lashing with a desperate accompaniment of fierce facial expressions, bristling whiskers, and emphatic gestures. I love this brave fellow creature; but if he were only a few inches bigger, I should never risk my life in his woods without a gun.

This is a beautiful world, and all who go out under the open sky will feel the gentle, kindly influence of Nature and hear her good tidings. The forests of the earth are the flags of Nature. They appeal to all and awaken inspiring universal feelings. Enter the forest and the boundaries of nations are forgotten. It may be that some time an immortal pine will be the flag of a united and peaceful world.

A Watcher on the Heights

A Watcher on the Heights

WHILE on the sky-line as State Snow Observer, I had one adventure with the elements that called for the longest special report that I have ever written. Perhaps I cannot do better than quote this report transmitted to Professor Carpenter, at Denver, on May 26, 1904.

NOTES ON THE POUDRE FLOOD

The day before the Poudre flood, I traveled for eight hours northwesterly along the top of the Continental Divide, all the time being above timber-line and from eleven thousand to twelve thousand feet above sea-level.

The morning was cloudless and hot. The western sky was marvelously clear. Eastward, a thin, dark haze overspread everything below ten thousand feet. By 9.30 A. M. this haze had ascended higher than where I was. At nine o'clock the snow on which I walked, though it had been

83

frozen hard during the night, was soggy and wet.

About 9.30 a calm that had prevailed all the morning gave way before an easy intermittent warm breeze from the southeast.

At 10.10 the first cloud appeared in the north, just above Hague's Peak. It was a heavy cumulus cloud, but I do not know from what direction it came. It rose high in the air, drifted slowly toward the west, and then seemed to dissolve. At any rate, it vanished. About 10.30 several heavy clouds rose from behind Long's Peak, moving toward the northwest, rising higher into the sky as they advanced.

The wind, at first in fitful dashes from the southeast, began to come more steadily and swiftly after eleven o'clock, and was so warm that the snow softened to a sloppy state. The air carried a tinge of haze, and conditions were oppressive. It was labor to breathe. Never, except one deadly hot July day in New York City, have I felt so overcome with heat and choking air. Perspiration simply streamed from me. These oppressive conditions continued for two hours,—

ON THE HEIGHTS

until about one o'clock. While they lasted, my eyes pained, ached, and twitched. There was no ,lare, but only by keeping my eyes closed could I stand the half-burning pain. Finally I came to some crags and lay down for a time in the shade. I was up eleven thousand five hundred feet and the time was 12.20. As I lay on the snow gazing upward, I became aware that there were several flotillas of clouds of from seven to twenty each, and these were moving toward every point of the compass. Each seemed on a different stratum of air, and each moved through space a considerable distance above or below the others. The clouds moving eastward were the highest. Most of the lower clouds were those moving westward. The haze and sunlight gave color to every cloud, and this color varied from smoky red to orange.

At two o'clock the haze came in from the east almost as dense as a fog-bank, crossed the ridge before me, and spread out as dark and foreboding as the smoke of Vesuvius. Behind me the haze rolled upward when it struck the ridge, and I had clear glimpses whenever I looked to the southwest. This heavy, muddy haze prevailed for a little more than half an hour, and as it cleared, the clouds began to disappear, but a gauzy haze still continued in the air. The feeling in the air was not agreeable, and for the first time in my life I felt alarmed by the shifting, rioting clouds and the weird haze.

I arrived at timber-line south of Poudre Lakes about 4.30 P. M., and for more than half an hour the sky, except in the east over the foothills, was clear, and the sunlight struck a glare from the snow. With the cleared air there came to me an easier feeling. The oppressiveness ceased. I descended a short distance into the woods and relaxed on a fallen tree that lay above the snow.

I had been there but a little while, when — snap! buzz! buzz! buzz! ziz! ziz! and electricity began to pull my hair and hum around my ears. The electricity passed off shortly, but in a little while it caught me again by the hair for a brief time, and this time my right arm momentarily cramped and my heart seemed to give several lurches. I arose and tramped on and downward, but every little while I was in for shocking treat-

ment. The electrical waves came from the southwest and moved northeast. They were separated
by periods of from one to several minutes in
length, and were about two seconds in passing.
During their presence they made it lively for me,
with hair-pulling, heart-palpitation, and muscular
cramps. I tried moving speedily with the wave,
also standing still and lying down, hoping that
the wave would pass me by; but in each and
every case it gave me the same stirring treatment. Once I stood erect and rigid as the wave
came on, but it intensified suddenly the rigidity
of every muscle to a seemingly rupturing extent,
and I did not try that plan again. The effect of
each wave on me seemed to be slightly weak-
ened whenever I lay down and fully relaxed my
muscles.

I was on a northerly slope, in spruce timber,
tramping over five feet of snow. During these
electrical waves, the points of dry twigs were
tipped with a smoky blue flame, and sometimes
bands of this bluish flame encircled green trees
just below their lower limbs. I looked at the
compass a few times, and though the needle

occasionally swayed a little, it was not affected in any marked manner.

The effect of the electrical waves on me became less as I descended, but whether from my getting below the electrical stratum, or from a cessation of the current, I cannot say.

But I did not descend much below eleven thousand feet, and at the lowest point I crossed the South Poudre, at the outlet of Poudre Lakes. In crossing I broke through the ice and received a wetting, with the exception of my right side above the hip. Once across, I walked about two hundred yards through an opening, then again entered the woods, on the southeasterly slope of Specimen Mountain. I had climbed only a short distance up this slope when another electrical wave struck me. The effect of this was similar to that of the preceding ones. There was, however, a marked difference in the intensity with which the electricity affected the wet and the dry portions of my body. The effect on my right side and shoulder, which had escaped wetting when I broke through the ice, was noticeably stronger than on the rest of my body. Climbing soon dried my clothes sufficiently to make this difference no longer noticeable. The waves became more frequent than at first, but not so strong. I made a clumsy climb of about five hundred feet, my muscles being "muscle-bound" all the time with rigidity from electricity. But this climb brought me almost to timber-line on Specimen Mountain, and also under the shadow of the south peak of it. At this place the electrical effects almost ceased. Nor did I again seriously feel the current until I found myself out in the sunlight which came between the two peaks of Specimen. While I continued in the sunlight I felt the electrical wave, but, strange to say, when I again entered the shadow I almost wholly escaped it.

When I started on the last slope toward the top of North Specimen, I came out into the sunlight again, and I also passed into an electrical sea. The slope was free from snow, and as the electrical waves swept in close succession, about thirty seconds apart, they snapped, hummed, and buzzed in such a manner that their advance and retreat could be plainly heard. In passing by me, the noise was more of a crackling and humming nature, while a million faint sparks flashed from the stones (porphyry and rhyolite) as the wave passed over. But the effect on me became constant. Every muscle was almost immovable. I could climb only a few steps without weakening to the stopping-point. I breathed only by gasps, and my heart became violent and feeble by turns. I felt as if cinched in a steel corset. After I had spent ten long minutes and was only half-way up a slope, the entire length of which I had more than once climbed in a few minutes and in fine shape, I turned to retreat, but as there was no cessation of the electrical colic, I faced about and started up again. I reached the top a few minutes before 6.30 P. M., and shortly afterward the sun disappeared behind clouds and peaks.

I regret that I failed to notice whether the electrical effects ceased with the setting of the sun, but it was not long after the disappearance of the sun before I was at ease, enjoying the magnificent mountain-range of clouds that had formed above the foothills and stood up glorious in the sunlight.

A Watcher on the Heights

Shortly before five o'clock the clouds had begun to pile up in the east, and their gigantic forms, flowing outlines, and glorious lighting were the only things that caused the electrical effects to be forgotten even momentarily. The clouds formed into a long, solid, rounded range that rose to great height and was miles in length. The southern end of this range was in the haze, and I could not make out its outline further south than a point about opposite Loveland, Colorado, nor could I see the northern end beyond a few miles north of Cheyenne, where it was cut off by a dozen strata of low clouds that moved steadily at a right angle to the east. Sixty miles of length was visible. Its height, like that of the real mountains which it paralleled, diminished toward the north. The place of greatest altitude was about twenty-five miles distant from me. From my location, the clouds presented a long and smoothly terraced slope, the top of which was at least five thousand feet and may have been fifteen thousand feet above me. The clouds seemed compact; at times they surged upwards; then they would settle with a long, undulating swell, as if some unseen power were trying to force them further up the mountains, while they were afraid to try it. Finally a series of low, conical peaks rose on the summit of the cloud-range, and the peaks and the upper cloud-slope resembled the upper portion of a circus-tent. There were no rough places or angles.

When darkness came on, the surface of this cloud-range was at times splendidly illuminated by electricity beneath; and, when the darkness deepened, the electrical play beneath often caused the surface to shine momentarily like incandescent glass, and occasionally sinuous rivers of gold ran over the slopes. Several times I thought that the course of these golden rivers of electrical fire was from the bottom upward, but so brilliant and dazzling were they that I could not positively decide on the direction of their movement. Never have I seen such enormous cloudforms or such brilliant electrical effects.

The summit of Specimen Mountain, from which I watched the clouds and electrical flashes, is about twelve thousand five hundred feet above sea-level. A calm prevailed while I remained on top. It was about 8.30 P. M. when I left the summit, on snowshoes, and swept down the steep northern slope into the woods. This hurry caused no unusual heart or muscle action.

The next morning was cloudy as low down as ten thousand five hundred feet, and, for all I know, lower still. The night had been warm, and the morning had the oppressive feeling that dominated the morning before. The clouds broke up before nine o'clock, and the air, with haze in it, seemed yellow. About 10.30, haze and, soon after, clouds came in from the southeast (at this time I was high up on the southerly slope of Mt. Richthofen), and by eleven o'clock the sky was cloudy. Up to this time the air, when my snow-glasses were off, burned and twitched my eyes in the same manner as on the previous morning.

Early in the afternoon I left Grand Ditch Camp and started down to Chambers Lake. I had not gone far when drops of rain began to fall from time to time, and shortly after this my muscles began to twitch occasionally under electrical ticklings. At times slight muscular rigidity was noticeable. Just before two o'clock the clouds began to burst through between the trees. I was at an altitude of about eleven thousand feet and a short distance from the head of Trap Creek. Rain, hail, and snow fell in turn, and the lightning began frequently to strike the rocks. With the beginning of the lightning my muscles ceased to be troubled with either twitching or rigidity. For the two hours between 2 and 4 P. M. the crash and roll of thunder was incessant. I counted twenty-three times that the lightning struck the rocks, but I did not see it strike a tree. The clouds were low, and the wind came from the east and the northeast, then from the west.

About four o'clock, I broke through the snow, tumbled into Trap Creek, and had to swim a little. This stream was really very swift, and ran in a narrow gulch, but it was blocked by snow and by tree-limbs swept down by the flood, and a pond had been formed. It was crowded with a deep deposit of snow which rested on a shelf of ice. This covering was shattered and uplifted by the swollen stream, and I had slipped on the top of the gulch and tumbled in. Once in, the swift water tugged at me to pull me under; the cakes

A STORM ON THE ROCKIES

of snow and ice hampered me, and my snow-shoes were entangled with brush and limbs. The combination seemed determined to drown me. For a few seconds I put forth all my efforts to get at my pocket-knife. This accomplished, the fastenings of my snowshoes were cut, and unhampered by these, I escaped the waters.

Since I have felt no ill results, the effect of the entire experience may have been beneficial. The clouds, glorious as they had been in forma-tion and coloring, resulted in a terrible cloud-burst. Enormous quantities of water were poured out, and this, falling upon the treeless foothills, rushed away to do more than a million dollars' damage in the rich and beautiful Poudre Valley.

Climbing Long's Peak

Climbing Long's Peak

AMONG the best days that I have had outdoors are the two hundred and fifty-seven that were spent as a guide on Long's Peak. One day was required from the starting-place near my cabin for each round trip to the summit of the peak. Something of interest occurred to enliven each one of these climbs: a storm, an accident, the wit of some one or the enthusiasm of all the climbers. But the climb I remember with greatest satisfaction is the one on which I guided Harriet Peters, an eight-year-old girl, to the top.

It was a cold morning when we started for the top, but it was this day or wait until next season, for Harriet was to start for her Southern home in a day or two and could not wait for a more favorable morning. Harriet had spent the two preceding summers near my cabin, and around it had played with the chipmunks and ridden the burros, and she had made a few climbs with me up through the woods. We often talked of going to the top of Long's Peak when she should become strong enough to do so. This time came just after her eighth birthday. As I was as eager to have her make the climb as she was to make it, we started up the next morning after her aunt had given permission for her to go. She was happy when I lifted her at last into the saddle, away up on old "Top's" back. She was so small that I still wonder how she managed to stay on, but she did so easily.

Long's Peak is not only one of the most scenic of the peaks in the Rocky Mountains, but it is probably the most rugged. From our starting-place it was seven miles to the top; five of these miles may be ridden, but the last two are so steep and craggy that one must go on foot and climb.

After riding a little more than a mile, we came to a clear, cold brook that is ever coming down in a great hurry over a steep mountain-side, splashing, jumping, and falling over the boulders of one of nature's stony stairways and forming white cascades which throw their spray among the tall, dark pines. I had told Harriet that ouzels

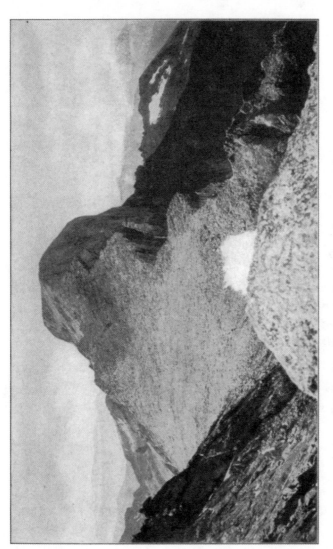

LONG'S PEAK FROM THE SUMMIT OF MT. MEEKER

lived by this brook; she was eager to see one, and we stopped at a promising place by the brook to watch. In less than a minute one came flying down the cascades, and so near to the surface of the water that he seemed to be tumbling and sliding down with it. He alighted on a boulder near us, made two or three pleasant curtsies, and started to sing one of his low, sweet songs. He was doing the very thing of which I had so often told Harriet. We watched and listened with breathless interest. In the midst of the song he dived into the brook; in a moment he came up with a water-bug in his bill, settled on the boulder again, gave his nods, and resumed his song, seemingly at the point where he left off. After a few low, sweet notes he broke off again and plunged into the water. This time he came up quickly and alighted on the spot he had just left, and went on with his song without any preliminaries and as if there had been no interruption.

The water-ouzel is found by the alpine lakes and brooks on the mountains of the West. It is a modest-appearing bird, about the size of a thrush, and wears a plain dress of slaty blue.

This dress is finished with a tail-piece somewhat like that of the wren, though it is not upturned so much. The bird seems to love cascades, and often nests by one. It also shows its fondness for water by often flying along the brook, following every bend and break made by the stream, keeping close to the water all the time and frequently touching it. Over the quiet reaches it goes skimming; it plunges over the waterfalls, alights on rocks in the rapids, goes dashing through the spray, its every movement showing the ecstasies of eager life and joy in the hurrying water. Our ouzel was quietly feeding on the edge of the brook, when Harriet said good-bye as our ponies started up the trail.

Harriet had never been in school, but she could read, write, and sing. She had good health, and a brighter, cheerier little girl I have never seen. As we rode up the trail through the woods, the gray Douglas squirrels were busy with the harvest. They were cutting off and storing cones for winter food. In the treetops these squirrels seemed to be bouncing and darting in all directions. One would cut off a cone, then dart to the

next, and so swiftly that cones were constantly
dropping. Frequently the cones struck limbs and
bounded as they fell, often coming to the ground
to bounce and roll some distance over the forest floor. An occasional one went rolling and
bouncing down the steep mountain-side with
two or three happy chipmunks in jolly pursuit.

We watched one squirrel stow cones under
trash and in holes in the thick beds of needles.
These cones were buried near a tree, in a dead
limb of which the squirrel had a hole and a home.
Harriet asked many questions concerning the
cones, — why they were buried, how the squirrel
found them when they were buried in the snow,
and what became of those which were left buried.
I told her that during the winter the squirrel
came down and dug through the snow to the
cones and then fed upon the nuts. I also told
her that squirrels usually buried more cones than
were eaten. The uneaten cones, being left in the
ground, were in a way planted, and the nuts in
them in time sprouted, and young trees came
peeping up among the fallen leaves. The squirrel's way of observing Arbor Day makes him a

useful forester. Harriet said she would tell all her boy and girl friends what she knew of this squirrel's tree-planting ways, and would ask her uncle not to shoot the little tree-planter.

As we followed the trail up through the woods, I told Harriet many things concerning the trees, and the forces which influenced their distribution and growth. While we were traveling westward in the bottom of a gulch, I pointed out to her that the trees on the mountain that rose on the right and sloped toward the south were of a different kind from those on the mountain-side which rose on our left and sloped toward the north. After traveling four miles and climbing up two thousand feet above our starting-place, and, after from time to time coming to and passing kinds of trees which did not grow lower down the slopes, we at last came to timber-line, above which trees did not grow at all.

In North America between timber-line on the Rockies, at an altitude of about eleven thousand feet, and sea-level on the Florida coast, there are about six hundred and twenty kinds of trees and shrubs growing. Each kind usually grows in the

soil and clime that is best suited to its requirements; in other words, most trees are growing
where they can do the best, or where they can
do better than any other kind. Some trees do
the best at the moist seashore; some thrive in
swamps; others live only on the desert's edge;
some live on the edge of a river; and still others
manage to endure the storms of bleak heights.

At timber-line the trees have a hard time of
it. All of them at this place are dwarfed, many
distorted, some crushed to the earth, flattened out
upon the ground like pressed flowers, by the
snowdrifts that have so long lain upon them.
The winter winds at this place blow almost constantly from the same quarter for days at a time,
and often attain a high velocity. The effect of
these winds is strikingly shown by the trees.
None of the trees are tall, and most of them are
leaning, pushed partly over by the wind. Some
are sprawled on the ground like uncouth vines
or spread out from the stump like a fan with the
onsweeping direction of the storms. Most of the
standing, unsheltered trees have limbs only on
the leeward quarter, all the other limbs having

been blown off by the wind or cut off by the wind-blown gravel. Most of the exposed trees are destitute of bark on the portion of the trunk that faces these winter winds. Some of the dead standing trees are carved into strange totem-poles by the sand-blasts of many fierce storms. With all the trees warped or distorted, the effect of timber-line is weird and strange.

Harriet and I got off the ponies the better to examine some of the storm-beaten trees. Harriet was attracted to a few dwarf spruces that were standing in a drift of recently fallen snow. Although these dwarfed little trees were more than a hundred years old, they were so short that the little mountain-climber who stood by them was taller than they. After stroking one of the trees with her hand, Harriet stood for a time in silence, then out of her warm childish nature she said, "What brave little trees to live up here where they have to stand all the time in the snow!" Timber-line, with its strange tree statuary and treeless snowy peaks and crags rising above it, together with its many kinds of bird and animal life and its flower-fringed snowdrifts, is one of nature's most expressive exhibits, and I wish every one might visit it. At an altitude of about eleven thousand seven hundred feet we came to the last tree. It was ragged, and so small that you could have hidden it beneath a hat. It nestled up to a boulder, and appeared so cold and pitiful that Harriet wanted to know if it was lost. It certainly appeared as if it had been lost for a long, long time.

Among the crags Harriet and I kept sharp watch for mountain sheep, but we did not see any. We were fortunate enough, however, to see a flock of ptarmigan. These birds were huddled in a hole which narrowly escaped being trampled on by Top. They walked quietly away, and we had a good look at them. They were almost white; in winter they are pure white, while in summer they are of a grayish brown. At all times their dress matches the surroundings fairly well, so that they have a protective coloring which makes it difficult for their enemies to see them.

At an altitude of twelve thousand five hundred feet the horses were tied to boulders and left behind. From this place to the top of the peak the way is too rough or precipitous for horses. For a mile Harriet and I went forward over the boulders of an old moraine. The last half-mile was the most difficult of all; the way was steep and broken, and was entirely over rocks, which were covered with a few inches of snow that had fallen during the night.

We climbed slowly; all good climbers go slowly. Harriet also faithfully followed another good mountain rule, — "Look before you step." She did not fall, slip, or stumble while making the climb. Of course we occasionally rested, and whenever we stopped near a flat rock or a level place, we made use of it by lying down on our backs, straightening out arms and legs, relaxing every muscle, and for a time resting as loosely as possible. Just before reaching the top, we made a long climb through the deepest snow that we had encountered. Though the sun was warm, the air, rocks, and snow were cold. Not only was the snow cold to the feet, but climbing through it was tiresome, and at the first convenient place we stopped to rest. Finding a large, smooth rock, we lay down on our backs side by side. We talked for a time and watched an eagle soaring around up in the blue sky. I think Harriet must have recalled a suggestion which I made at timber-line, for without moving she suddenly remarked, " Mr. Mills, my feet are so cold that I can't tell whether my toes are wiggling or not."

Five hours after starting, Harriet stepped upon the top, the youngest climber to scale Long's Peak. The top is fourteen thousand two hundred and fifty-nine feet above the sea, is almost level, and, though rough, is roomy enough for a baseball game. Of course if the ball went over the edge, it would tumble a mile or so before stopping. With the top so large, you will realize that the base measures miles across. The upper three thousand feet of the peak is but a gigantic mass, almost destitute of soil or vegetation. Some of the rocks are flecked and spotted with lichens, and a few patches of moss and straggling, beautiful alpine flowers can be found during August. There is but little chance for snow to lodge, and for nearly three thousand feet the peak rises a bald, broken, impressive stone tower.

While Harriet and I were eating luncheon, a

ground-hog that I had fed on other visits came out to see if there was anything for him. Some sparrows also lighted near; they looked hungry, so we left some bread for them and then climbed upon the "tip-top," where our picture was taken.

From the tip-top we could see more than a hundred miles toward any point of the compass. West of us we saw several streams that were flowing away toward the Pacific; east of us the streams flowed to the Atlantic. I told Harriet that the many small streams we saw all grew larger as they neared the sea. Harriet lived at the "big" end of the Arkansas River. She suddenly wanted to know if I could show her the "little end of the Arkansas River."

After an hour on top we started downward and homeward, the little mountain-climber feeling happy and lively. But she was careful, and only once during the day did she slip, and this slip was hardly her fault: we were coming off an enormous smooth boulder that was wet from the new snow that was melting, when both Harriet's feet shot from under her and she fell, laughing, into my arms.

ON THE TIP-TOP OF LONG'S PEAK

Climbing Long's Peak

" Hello, Top, I am glad to see you," said Harriet when we came to the horses. While riding homeward I told Harriet that I had often climbed the peak by moonlight. On the way down she said good-bye to the little trees at timber-line, the squirrels, and the ouzel. When I at last lifted Harriet off old Top at the cabin, many people came out to greet her. To all she said, " Yes, I 'm tired, but some time I want to go up by moonlight."

Midget, the Return Horse

Midget, the Return Horse

IN many of the Western mining-towns, the liverymen keep "return horses," — horses that will return to the barn when set at liberty, whether near the barn or twenty miles away. These horses are the pick of their kind. They have brains enough to take training readily, and also to make plans of their own and get on despite the unexpected hindrances that sometimes occur. When a return horse is ridden to a neighboring town, he must know enough to find his way back, and he must also be so well trained that he will not converse too long with the horse he meets going in the opposite direction.

The return horse is a result of the necessities of mountain sections, especially the needs of miners. Most Western mining-towns are located upon a flat or in a gulch. The mines are rarely near the town, but are on the mountain-slopes above it. Out of town go a dozen roads or trails that extend to the mines, from one to five miles away, and much higher than the town. A miner does not mind walking down to the town, but he wants to ride back; or the prospector comes in and wants to take back a few supplies. The miner hires a return horse, rides it to the mine, and then turns the horse loose. It at once starts to return to the barn. If a horse meets a freight wagon coming up, it must hunt for a turnout if the road is narrow, and give the wagon the right of way. If the horse meets some one walking up, it must avoid being caught.

The San Juan mining section of southwestern Colorado has hundreds of these horses. Most of the mines are from one thousand to three thousand feet above the main supply-points, Ouray, Telluride, and Silverton. Ouray and Telluride are not far apart by trail, but they are separated by a rugged range that rises more than three thousand feet above them. Men often go by trail from one of these towns to the other, and in so doing usually ride a return horse to the top of the range, then walk down the other side.

"Be sure to turn Jim loose before you reach

A MINER ON A RETURN HORSE

the summit; he won't come back if you ride him even a short distance on the other side," called a Telluride liveryman to me as I rode out of his barn. It seems that the most faithful return horse may not come back if ridden far down the slope away from home, but may stray down it rather than climb again to the summit to return home. The rider is warned also to "fasten up the reins and see that the cinches are tight" when he turns the horse loose. If the cinches are loose, the saddle may turn when the horse rolls; or if the reins are down, the horse may graze for hours. Either loose reins or loose cinches may cripple a horse by entangling his feet, or by catching on a snag in the woods. Once loose, the horse generally starts off home on a trot. But he is not always faithful. When a number of these horses are together, they will occasionally play too long on the way. A great liking for grass sometimes tempts them into a ditch, where they may eat grass even though the reins are up.

The lot of a return horse is generally a hard one. A usurper occasionally catches a horse and rides him far away. Then, too often, his owner blames him for the delay, and for a time gives him only half-feed to "teach him not to fool along." Generally the return horse must also be a good snow horse, able to flounder and willing to make his way through deep drifts. He may be thirsty on a warm day, but he must go all the way home before having a drink. Often, in winter, he is turned loose at night on some bleak height to go back over a lonely trail, a task which he does not like. Horses, like most animals and like man, are not at ease when alone. A fallen tree across the trail or deepened snow sometimes makes the horse's return journey a hard one. On rare occasions, cinch or bridle gets caught on a snag or around his legs, and cripples him or entangles him so that he falls a victim to the unpitying mountain lion or some other carnivorous animal.

I have never met a return horse without stopping to watch it as far as it could be seen. They always go along with such unconscious confidence and quiet alertness that they are a delight to behold. Many good days I have had in their company, and on more than one occasion their

alertness, skill, and strength have saved me either
from injury or from the clutches of that great
white terror the snow-slide.

The February morning that I rode "Midget"
out of Alma began what proved to be by far
the most delightful association that I have ever
had with a return horse, and one of the happiest
experiences with nature and a dumb animal that
has ever come into my life.

I was in government experiment work as "State
Snow Observer," and wanted to make some observations on the summit peaks of the "Twelve-
Mile" and other ranges. Midget was to carry me
far up the side of these mountains to the summit
of Hoosier Pass. A heavy snow had fallen a few
days before I started out. The wind had drifted
most of this out of the open and piled it deeply
in the woods and gulches. Midget galloped merrily away over the wind-swept ground. We came
to a gulch, I know not how deep, that was filled
with snow, and here I began to appreciate
Midget. Across this gulch it was necessary for
us to go. The snow was so deep and so soft that
I dismounted and put on my snowshoes and

Wild Life on the Rockies

started to lead Midget across. She followed willingly. After a few steps, a flounder and a snort caused me to look back, and all I could see of Midget was her two little ears wriggling in the snow. When we reached the other side, Midget came out breathing heavily, and at once shook her head to dislodge the snow from her forehead and her ears. She was impatient to go on, and before I could take off my snowshoes and strap them on my back, she was pawing the ground impatiently, first with one little fore foot and then with the other. I leaped into the saddle and away we went again. We had a very pleasant morning of it.

About eleven o'clock I dismounted to take a picture of the snowy slope of Mt. Silverheels. Evidently Midget had never before seen a kodak. She watched with extraordinary interest the standing of the little three-legged affair upon the ground and the mounting of the small black box upon it. She pointed her ears at it; tilted her head to one side and moved her nose up and down. I moved away from her several feet to take the picture. She eyed the kodak with such intentness that I invited her to come over and have a look at it. She came at once, turning her head and neck to one side to prevent the bridle-reins, which I had thrown upon the ground, from entangling her feet. Once by me, she looked the kodak and tripod over with interest, smelled of them, but was careful not to strike the tripod with her feet or to overturn it and the kodak with her nose. She seemed so interested that I told her all about what I was doing, — what I was taking a picture of, why I was taking it, and how long an exposure I was going to give it; and finally I said to her: "To-morrow, Midget, when you are back in your stall in the barn at Alma, eating oats, I shall be on the other side of Mt. Silverheels, taking pictures there. Do you understand?" She pawed the ground with her right fore foot with such a satisfied look upon her face that I was sure she thought she understood all about it.

From time to time I took other pictures, and after the first experience Midget did not wait to be invited to come over and watch me, but always followed me to every new spot where I set the tripod and kodak down, and on each occasion I talked freely with her, and she seemed to understand and to be much interested.

Shortly after noon, when I was taking a picture, Midget managed to get her nose into my mammoth outside coat-pocket. There she found something to her liking. It was my habit to eat lightly when rambling about the mountains, often eating only once a day, and occasionally going two or three days without food. I had a few friends who were concerned about me, and who were afraid I might some time starve to death. So, partly as a joke and partly in earnest, they would mail me a package of something to eat, whenever they knew at what post-office I was likely to turn up. At Alma, the morning I hired Midget, the prize package which I drew from the post-office contained salted peanuts. I did not care for them, but put them into my pocket. It was past noon and Midget was hungry. I was chattering away to her about picture-taking when, feeling her rubbing me with her nose, I put my hand around to find that she was eating salted peanuts from my big coat-pocket. Midget enjoyed them so much that I allowed her to put her nose into my pocket and help herself, and from time to time, too, I gave her a handful of them until they were all gone.

Late in the afternoon, Midget and I arrived at the top of Hoosier Pass. I told her to look tired and I would take her picture. She dropped her head and neck a little, and there on the wind-swept pass, with the wind-swept peaks in the background, I photographed her. Then I told her it was time to go home, that it was sure to be after dark before she could get back. So I tightened the cinches, fastened up the bridle-rein over the horn of the saddle, and told her to go. She looked around at me, but did not move. Evidently she preferred to stay with me. So I spoke to her sternly and said, "Midget, you will have to go home!" Without even looking round, she kicked up her heels and trotted speedily down the mountain and disappeared. I did not imagine that we would meet again for some time.

I went on, and at timber-line on Mt. Lincoln I built a camp-fire and without bedding spent the night by it. The next day I climbed several peaks, took many photographs, measured many snow-drifts, and made many notes in my notebook. When night came on, I descended from the crags and snows into the woods, built a fire, and spent the night by it, sleeping for a little while at a time. Awakening with the cold, I would get up and revive my fire, and then lie down to sleep. The next day a severe storm came on, and I was compelled to huddle by my fire all day, for the wind was so fierce and the snow so blinding that it would have been extremely risky to try to cross the craggy and slippery mountain-summits. All that day I stayed by the fire, but that night, instead of trying to get a little sleep there, I crawled into a newly formed snowdrift, and in it slept soundly and quite comfortably until morning. Toward noon the storm ceased, but it had delayed me a day. I had brought with me only a pound of raisins, and had eaten these during the first two days. I felt rather hungry, and almost wished I had saved some of the salted peanuts that I had given Midget, but I felt fresh and vigorous, and joyfully I made my way over the snowy crest of the continent.

Midget, the Return Horse

Late that night I came into the mining-town of Leadville. At the hotel I found letters and a telegram awaiting me. This telegram told me that it was important for me to come to the Pike's Peak National Forest at the earliest possible moment.

After a light supper and an hour's rest, I again tied on my snowshoes, and at midnight started to climb. The newly fallen snow on the steep mountain-side was soft and fluffy. I sank so deeply into it and made such slow progress that it was late in the afternoon of the next day before I reached timber-line on the other side. The London mine lay a little off my course, and knowing that miners frequently rode return horses up to it, I thought that by going to the mine I might secure a return horse to carry me back to Alma, which was about thirteen miles away. With this in mind, I started off in a hurry. In my haste I caught one of my webbed shoes on the top of a gnarly, storm-beaten tree that was buried and hidden in the snow. I fell, or rather dived, into the snow, and in so doing broke a snowshoe and lost my hat. This affair delayed me a little, and I gave up going

125

to the mine, but concluded to go to the trail about a mile below it, and there intercept the first return horse that came down. Just before I reached the trail, I heard a horse coming.

As this trail was constantly used, the snow was packed down, while the untrampled snow on each side of it lay from two to four feet deep. Seeing that this pony was going to get past before I could reach the trail, I stopped, took a breath, and called out to it. When I said, "Hello, pony," the pony did not hello. Instead of slackening its pace, it seemed to increase it. Knowing that this trail was one that Midget had often to cover, I concluded as a forlorn hope to call her name, thinking that the pony might be Midget. So I called out, "Hello, Midget!" The pony at once stopped, looked all around, and gave a delighted little whinny. It was Midget! The instant she saw me, she tried to climb up out of the trail into the deep snow where I was, but I hastened to prevent her. Leaping down by her side, I put my arm around her neck, and told her that I was very glad to see her, and that I wanted to ride to Alma. Her nose found its way into my coat-pocket. "Well, Midget, it is too bad. Really, I was not expecting to see you, and I have n't a single salted peanut, but if you will just allow me to ride this long thirteen miles into Alma, I will give you all the salted peanuts that you will be allowed to eat. I am tired, and should very much like to have a ride. Will you take me?" She at once started to paw the snowy trail with a small fore foot, as much as to say, "Hurry up!" I took off my snowshoes, and without waiting to fasten them on my back, jumped into the saddle. In a surprisingly short time, and with loud stamping on the floor, Midget carried me into the livery barn at Alma.

When her owner saw a man in the saddle, he was angry, and reminded me that it was unfair and illegal to capture a return horse; but when he recognized me, he at once changed his tone, and he became friendly when I told him that Midget had invited me to ride. He said that as she had invited me to ride I should have to pay the damages to her. I told him that we had already agreed to this. "But how in thunder did you catch her?" he asked. "Yesterday Pat O'Brien

127

tried that, and he is now in the hospital with two broken ribs. She kicked him."

I said good-bye to Midget, and went to my supper, leaving her contentedly eating salted peanuts.

Faithful Scotch

Faithful Scotch

I CARRIED little Scotch all day long in my over-coat pocket as I rode through the mountains on the way to my cabin. His cheerful, cunning face, his good behavior, and the clever way in which he poked his head out of my pocket, licked my hand, and looked at the scenery, completely won my heart before I had ridden an hour. That night he showed so strikingly the strong, faith-ful characteristics for which collies are noted that I resolved never to part with him. Since then we have had great years together. We have been hungry and happy together, and together we have played by the cabin, faced danger in the wilds, slept peacefully among the flowers, fol-lowed the trails by starlight, and cuddled down in winter's drifting snow.

On my way home through the mountains with puppy Scotch, I stopped for a night near a de-serted ranch-house and shut him up in a small abandoned cabin. He at once objected and set up a terrible barking and howling, gnawing

fiercely at the crack beneath the door and trying to tear his way out. Fearing he would break
his little puppy teeth, or possibly die from frantic
and persistent efforts to be free, I concluded to
release him from the cabin. My fears that he
would run away if left free were groundless. He
made his way to my saddle, which lay on the
ground near by, crawled under it, turned round
beneath it, and thrust his little head from beneath the arch of the horn and lay down with a
look of contentment, and also with an air which
said, " I 'll take care of this saddle. I 'd like to
see any one touch it."

And watch it he did. At midnight a cowboy
came to my camp-fire. He had been thrown from
his bronco and was making back to his outfit on
foot. In approaching the fire his path lay close
to my saddle, beneath which Scotch was lying.
Tiny Scotch flew at him ferociously; never have
I seen such faithful ferociousness in a dog so
small and young. I took him in my hands and
assured him that the visitor was welcome, and in
a moment little Scotch and the cowboy were side
by side gazing at the fire.

132

SCOTCH NEAR TIMBER-LINE

Faithful Scotch

I suppose his bravery and watchful spirit may be instinct inherited from his famous forbears who lived so long and so cheerfully on Scotland's heaths and moors. But, with all due respect for inherited qualities, he also has a brain that does a little thinking and meets emergencies promptly and ably.

He took serious objection to the coyotes which howled, serenaded, and made merry in the edge of the meadow about a quarter of a mile from my cabin. Just back of their howling-ground was a thick forest of pines, in which were scores of broken rocky crags. Into the tangled forest the coyotes always retreated when Scotch gave chase, and into this retreat he dared not pursue them. So long as the coyotes sunned themselves, kept quiet, and played, Scotch simply watched them contentedly from afar; but the instant they began to howl and yelp, he at once raced over and chased them into the woods. They often yelped and taunted him from their safe retreat, but Scotch always took pains to lie down on the edge of the open and remain there until they became quiet or went away.

During the second winter that Scotch was with me and before he was two years of age, one of the wily coyotes showed a tantalizing spirit and some interesting cunning which put Scotch on his mettle. One day when Scotch was busy driving the main pack into the woods, one that trotted lame with the right fore leg emerged from behind a rocky crag at the edge of the open and less than fifty yards from Scotch. Hurrying to a willow clump about fifty yards in Scotch's rear, he set up a broken chorus of yelps and howls, seemingly with delight and to the great annoyance of Scotch, who at once raced back and chased the noisy taunter into the woods.

The very next time that Scotch was chasing the pack away, the crippled coyote again sneaked from behind the crag, took refuge behind the willow clump, and began delivering a perfect shower of broken yelps. Scotch at once turned back and gave chase. Immediately the entire pack wheeled from retreat and took up defiant attitudes in the open, but this did not seem to trouble Scotch; he flung himself upon them with great ferocity, and finally drove them all back into the woods. However, the third time that the cunning coyote had come to his rear, the entire pack stopped in the edge of the open and, for a time, defied him. He came back from this chase panting and tired and carrying every expression of worry. It seemed to prey upon him to such an extent that I became a little anxious about him.

One day, just after this affair, I went for the mail, and allowed Scotch to go with me. I usually left him at the cabin, and he stayed unchained and was faithful, though it was always evident that he was anxious to go with me and also that he was exceedingly lonely when left behind. But on this occasion he showed such eagerness to go that I allowed him the pleasure.

At the post-office he paid but little attention to the dogs which, with their masters, were assembled there, and held himself aloof from them, squatting on the ground with head erect and almost an air of contempt for them, but it was evident that he was watching their every move. When I started homeward, he showed great satisfaction by leaping and barking.

That night was wildly stormy, and I concluded

to go out and enjoy the storm on some wind-swept crags. Scotch was missing and I called him, but he did not appear, so I went alone. After being tossed by the wind for more than an hour, I returned to the cabin, but Scotch was still away. This had never occurred before, so I concluded not to go to bed until he returned. He came home after daylight, and was accompanied by another dog, — a collie, which belonged to a rancher who lived about fifteen miles away. I remembered to have seen this dog at the post-office the day before. My first thought was to send the dog home, but I finally concluded to allow him to remain, to see what would come of his presence, for it was apparent that Scotch had gone for him. He appropriated Scotch's bed in the tub, to the evident satisfaction of Scotch. During the morning the two played together in the happiest possible manner for more than an hour. At noon I fed them together.

In the afternoon, while I was writing, I heard the varied voices of the coyote pack, and went out with my glass to watch proceedings, wondering how the visiting collie would play his part.

Faithful Scotch

There went Scotch, as I supposed, racing for the yelping pack, but the visiting collie was not to be seen. The pack beat the usual sullen, scattering retreat, and while the dog, which I supposed to be Scotch, was chasing the last slow tormenter into the woods, from behind the crag came the big limping coyote, hurrying toward the willow clump from behind which he was accustomed to yelp triumphantly in Scotch's rear. I raised the glass for a better look, all the time wondering where the visiting collie was keeping himself. I was unable to see him, yet I recollected he was with Scotch less than an hour before.

The lame coyote came round the willow clump as usual, and threw up his head as though to bay at the moon. Then the unexpected happened. On the instant, Scotch leaped into the air out of the willow clump, and came down upon the coyote's back! They rolled about for some time, when the coyote finally shook himself free and started at a lively limping pace for the woods, only to be grabbed again by the visiting collie, which had been chasing the pack, and which I had mistaken for Scotch. The pack beat a swift retreat. For a time both dogs fought the coyote fiercely, but he at last tore himself free, and escaped into the pines, badly wounded and bleeding. I never saw him again. That night the visiting collie went home. As Scotch was missing that night for a time, I think he may have accompanied him at least a part of the way.

One day a young lady from Michigan came along and wanted to climb Long's Peak all alone, without a guide. I agreed to consent to this if first she would climb one of the lesser peaks unaided, on a stormy day. This the young lady did, and by so doing convinced me that she had a keen sense of direction and an abundance of strength, for the day on which she climbed was a stormy one, and the peak was completely be-fogged with clouds. After this, there was nothing for me to do but allow her to climb Long's Peak alone.

Just as she was starting, that cool September morning, I thought to provide for an emergency by sending Scotch with her. He knew the trail well and would, of course, lead her the right way, providing she lost the trail. " Scotch," said I, " go

with this young lady, take good care of her, and
stay with her till she returns. Don't you desert
her." He gave a few barks of satisfaction and
started with her up the trail, carrying himself in
a manner which indicated that he was both honored and pleased. I felt that the strength and
alertness of the young lady, when combined with
the faithfulness and watchfulness of Scotch, would
make the journey a success, so I went about my
affairs as usual. When darkness came on that
evening, the young lady had not returned.

She climbed swiftly until she reached the rocky
alpine moorlands above timber-line. Here she lingered long to enjoy the magnificent scenery and
the brilliant flowers. It was late in the afternoon
when she arrived at the summit of the peak.
After she had spent a little time there resting and
absorbing the beauty and grandeur of the scene,
she started to return. She had not proceeded far
when clouds and darkness came on, and on a slope
of slide-rock she lost the trail.

Scotch had minded his own affairs and enjoyed
himself in his own way all day long. Most of the
time he followed her closely, apparently indifferent

to what happened, but when she, in the darkness, left the trail and started off in the wrong direction, he at once came forward, and took the lead with an alert, aggressive air. The way in which he did this should have suggested to the young lady that he knew what he was about, but she did not appreciate this fact. She thought he had become weary and wanted to run away from her, so she called him back. Again she started in the wrong direction; this time Scotch got in front of her and refused to move. She pushed him out of the way. Once more he started off in the right direction, and this time she scolded him and reminded him that his master had told him not to desert her. Scotch dropped his ears and sheepishly fell in behind her and followed meekly along. He had obeyed orders.

After traveling a short distance, the young lady realized that she had lost her way, but it never occurred to her that she had only to trust Scotch and he would lead her directly home. However, she had the good sense to stop where she was, and there, among the crags, by the stained remnants of winter's snow, thirteen thousand feet above sea-level, she was to spend the night. The cold wind blew a gale, roaring and booming among the crags, the alpine brooklet turned to ice, while, in the lee of the crag, shivering with cold, hugging shaggy Scotch in her arms, she lay down for the night.

I had given my word not to go in search of her if she failed to return. However, I sent out four guides to look for her. They suffered much from cold as they vainly searched among the crags through the dark hours of the windy night. Just at sunrise one of them found her, almost exhausted, but, with slightly frost-bitten fingers, still hugging Scotch in her arms. He gave her food and drink and additional wraps, and without delay started with her down the trail. As soon as she was taken in charge by the guide, patient Scotch left her and hurried home. He had saved her life.

Scotch's hair is long and silky, black with a touch of tawny about the head and a little bar of white on the nose. He has the most expressive and pleasing dog's face I have ever seen. There is nothing he enjoys so well as to have some one kick the football for him. For an hour at a time he will chase it and try to get hold of it, giving an occasional eager, happy bark. He has good eyes, and these, with his willingness to be of service, have occasionally made him useful to me in finding articles which I, or some one else, had forgotten or lost on the trail. Generally it is difficult to make him understand just what has been lost or where he is to look for it, but when once he understands, he keeps up the search, sometimes for hours if he does not find the article before. He is always faithful in guarding any object that I ask him to take care of. I have but to throw down a coat and point at it, and he will at once lie down near by, there to remain until I come to dismiss him. He will allow no one else to touch it. His attitude never fails to convey the impression that he would die in defense of the thing intrusted to him, but desert it or give it up, never!

One February day I took Scotch and started up Long's Peak, hoping to gain its wintry summit. Scotch easily followed in my snowshoe-tracks. At an altitude of thirteen thousand feet on the wind-swept steeps there was but little snow, and it was necessary to leave snowshoes behind. After climbing a short distance on these icy slopes, I became alarmed for the safety of Scotch. By and by I had to cut steps in the ice. This made the climb too perilous for him, as he could not realize the danger he was in should he miss a step. There were places where slipping from these steps meant death, so I told Scotch to go back. I did not, however, tell him to watch my snowshoes, for so dangerous was the climb that I did not know that I should ever get back to them myself. However, he went to the snowshoes, and with them he remained for eight cold hours until I came back by the light of the stars.

On a few occasions I allowed Scotch to go with me on short winter excursions. He enjoyed these immensely, although he had a hard time of it and but very little to eat. When we camped among the spruces in the snow, he seemed to enjoy sitting by my side and silently watching the evening fire, and he contentedly cuddled with me to keep warm at night.

Wild Life on the Rockies

One cold day we were returning from a four days' excursion when, a little above timber-line, I stopped to take some photographs. To do this it was necessary for me to take off my sheepskin mittens, which I placed in my coat-pocket, but not securely, as it proved. From time to time, as I climbed to the summit of the Continental Divide, I stopped to take photographs, but on the summit the cold pierced my silk gloves and I felt for my mittens, to find that one of them was lost. I stooped, put an arm around Scotch, and told him I had lost a mitten, and that I wanted him to go down for it to save me the trouble. "It won't take you very long, but it will be a hard trip for me. Go and fetch it to me." Instead of starting off hurriedly, willingly, as he had invariably done before in obedience to my commands, he stood still. His alert, eager ears drooped, but no other move did he make. I repeated the command in my most kindly tones. At this, instead of starting down the mountain for the mitten, he slunk slowly away toward home. It was clear that he did not want to climb down the steep icy slope of a mile to timber-line, more than a thousand feet

THE CLOUD-CAPPED CONTINENTAL DIVIDE

below. I thought he had misunderstood me, so I called him back, patted him, and then, pointing down the slope, said, "Go for the mitten, Scotch; I will wait here for you." He started for it, but went unwillingly. He had always served me so cheerfully that I could not understand, and it was not until late the next afternoon that I realized that he had not understood me, but that he had loyally, and at the risk of his life, tried to obey me.

The summit of the Continental Divide, where I stood when I sent him back, was a very rough and lonely region. On every hand were broken snowy peaks and rugged cañons. My cabin, eighteen miles away, was the nearest house to it, and the region was utterly wild. I waited a reasonable time for Scotch to return, but he did not come back. Thinking he might have gone by without my seeing him, I walked some distance along the summit, first in one direction and then in the other, but, seeing neither him nor his tracks, I knew that he had not yet come back. As it was late in the afternoon, and growing colder, I decided to go slowly on toward my cabin. I started along a route that I felt sure he would follow, and I reasoned that he would overtake me. Darkness came on and still no Scotch, but I kept going forward. For the remainder of the way I told myself that he might have got by me in the darkness.

When, at midnight, I arrived at the cabin, I expected to be greeted by him, but he was not there. I felt that something was wrong and feared that he had met with an accident. I slept two hours and rose, but still he was missing, so I concluded to tie on my snowshoes and go to meet him. The thermometer showed fourteen below zero.

I started at three o'clock in the morning, feeling that I should meet him without going far. I kept going on and on, and when, at noon, I arrived at the place on the summit from which I had sent him back, Scotch was not there to cheer the wintry, silent scene.

I slowly made my way down the slope, and at two in the afternoon, twenty-four hours after I had sent Scotch back, I paused on a crag and looked below. There in the snowy world of white he lay by the mitten in the snow. He had misunderstood me, and had gone back to guard the mitten instead of to get it. He could hardly contain himself for joy when he saw me. He leaped into the air, barked, jumped, rolled over, licked my hand, whined, grabbed the mitten, raced round and round me, and did everything that an alert, affectionate, faithful dog could do to show that he appreciated my appreciation of his supremely faithful services.

After waiting for him to eat a luncheon, we started merrily towards home, where we arrived at one o'clock in the morning. Had I not returned, I suppose Scotch would have died beside the mitten. In a region cold, cheerless, oppressive, without food, and perhaps to die, he lay down by the mitten because he understood that I had told him to. In the annals of dog heroism, I know of no greater deed.

Goß and Some Other Birds

Bob and Some Other Birds

BIRDS are plentiful on the Rockies, and the accumulating information concerning them may, in a few years, accredit Colorado with having more kinds of birds than any other State. The mountains and plains of Colorado carry a wide range of geographic conditions,—a variety of life-zones, — and in many places there is an abundance of bird-food of many kinds. These conditions naturally produce a large variety of birds throughout the State.

Notwithstanding this array of feathered inhabitants, most tourists who visit the West complain of a scarcity of birds. But birds the Rockies have, and any bird-student could tell why more of them are not seen by tourists. The loud manners of most tourists who invade the Rockies simply put the birds to flight. When I hear the approach of tourists in the wilds, I feel instinctively that I should fly for safety myself. " Our little brothers of the air " the world over dislike the crowd, and will linger only for those who come with deliberation and quiet.

This entire mountain-section, from foothills to mountain-summits, is enlivened in nesting-time with scores of species of birds. Low down on the foothills one will find Bullock's oriole, the red-headed woodpecker, the Arkansas kingbird, and one will often see, and more often hear, the clear, strong notes of the Western meadowlark ringing over the hills and meadows. The wise, and rather murderous, magpie goes chattering about. Here and there the quiet bluebird is seen. The kingfisher is in his appointed place. Long-crested jays, Clarke's crows, and pigmy nut-hatches are plentiful, and the wild note of the chickadee is heard on every hand. Above the altitude of eight thousand feet you may hear, in June, the marvelous melody of Audubon's hermit thrush.

Along the brooks and streams lives the water-ouzel. This is one of the most interesting and self-reliant of Rocky Mountain birds. It loves the swift, cool mountain-streams. It feeds in them, nests within reach of the splash of their spray, closely follows their bent and sinuous course in flight, and from an islanded boulder mingles its liquid song with the music of the moving waters. There is much in the life of the ouzel that is refreshing and inspiring. I wish it were better known.

Around timber-line in summer one may hear the happy song of the white-throated sparrow. Here and above lives the leucosticte. Far above the vanguard of the brave pines, where the brilliant flowers fringe the soiled remnants of winter's drifted snow, where sometimes the bees hum and the painted butterflies sail on easy wings, the broad-tailed hummingbird may occasionally be seen, while still higher the eagles soar in the quiet bending blue. On the heights, sometimes nesting at an altitude of thirteen thousand feet, is found the ptarmigan, which, like the Eskimo, seems supremely contented in the land of crags and snows.

Of all the birds on the Rockies, the one most marvelously eloquent is the solitaire. I have often felt that everything stood still and that every beast and bird listened while the matchless solitaire sang. The hermit thrush seems to suppress one, to give one a touch of reflective loneliness; but the solitaire stirs one to be up and doing, gives one the spirit of youth. In the solitaire's song one feels all the freshness and the promise of spring. The song seems to be born of ages of freedom beneath peaceful skies, of the rhythm of the universe, of a mingling of the melody of winds and waters and of all rhythmic sounds that murmur and echo out of doors and of every song that Nature sings in the wild gardens of the world. I am sure I have never been more thoroughly wide awake and hopeful than when listening to the solitaire's song. The world is flushed with a diviner atmosphere, every object carries a fresher significance, there are new thoughts and clear, calm hopes sure to be realized on the enchanted fields of the future. I was camping alone one evening in the deep solitude of the Rockies. The slanting sun-rays were glowing on St. Vrain's crag-crowned hills and everything was at peace, when, from a near-by treetop came the triumphant, hopeful song of a solitaire, and I forgot all except that the world was young. One believes in fairies when the solitaire sings. Some of my friends have predicted that I shall some time meet with an accident and perish in the solitudes alone. If their prediction should come true, I shall hope it will be in the summer-time, while the flowers are at their best, and that during my last conscious moments I shall hear the melody of the solitaire singing as I die with the dying day.

I sat for hours in the woods one day, watching a pair of chickadees feeding their young ones. There were nine of these hungry midgets, and, like nine small boys, they not only were always hungry, but were capable of digesting everything. They ate spiders and flies, green worms, ants, millers, dirty brown worms, insect-eggs by the dozen, devil's-darning-needles, woodlice, bits of lichen, grasshoppers, and I know not how many other things. I could not help thinking that when one family of birds destroyed such numbers of injurious insects, if all the birds were to stop eating, the insects would soon destroy every green tree and plant on earth.

One of the places where I used to camp to

enjoy the flowers, the trees, and the birds was on
the shore of a glacier lake. Near the lake were
eternal snows, rugged gorges, and forests primeval. To its shore, especially in autumn, came
many bird callers. I often screened myself in
a dense clump of fir trees on the north shore to
study the manners of birds which came near. To
help attract and detain them, I scattered feed
on the shore, and I spent interesting hours and
days in my hiding-place enjoying the etiquette of
birds at feast and frolic.

I was lying in the sun, one afternoon, just outside my fir clump, gazing out across the lake,
when a large black bird alighted on the shore
some distance around the lake. "Surely," I said
to myself, "that is a crow." A crow I had not
seen or heard of in that part of the country. I
wanted to call to him that he was welcome to
eat at my free-lunch counter, when it occurred
to me that I was in plain sight. Before I could
move, the bird rose in the air and started flying
leisurely toward me. I hoped he would see, or
smell, the feed and tarry for a time; but he rose
as he advanced, and as he appeared to be looking

ahead, I had begun to fear he would go by without stopping, when he suddenly wheeled and at the same instant said "Hurrah," as distinctly as I have ever heard it spoken, and dropped to the feed. The clearness, energy, and unexpectedness of his "Hurrah" startled me. He alighted and began to eat, evidently without suspecting my presence, notwithstanding the fact that I lay only a few feet away. Some days before, a mountain lion had killed a mountain sheep; a part of this carcass I had dragged to my bird table. Upon this the crow, for such he was, alighted and fed ravenously for some time. Then he paused, straightened up, and took a look about. His eye fell on me, and instantly he squatted as if to hurl himself in hurried flight, but he hesitated, then appeared as if starting to burst out with "Caw" or some such exclamation, but changed his mind and repressed it. Finally he straightened and fixed himself for another good look at me. I did not move, and my clothes must have been a good shade of protective coloring, for he seemed to conclude that I was not worth considering. He looked straight at me for a few seconds, uttered another "Hurrah," which he emphasized with a defiant gesture, and went on energetically eating. In the midst of this, something alarmed him, and he flew swiftly away and did not come back. Was this crow a pet that had concluded to strike out for himself? Or had his mimicry or his habit of laying hold of whatever pleased him caused him to appropriate this word from bigger folk?

Go where you will over the Rockies and the birds will be with you. One day I spent several hours on the summit of Long's Peak, and while there twelve species of birds alighted or passed near enough for me to identify them. One of these birds was an eagle, another a humming-bird.

On a June day, while the heights were more than half covered with winter's snow, I came across the nest of a ptarmigan near a drift and at an altitude of thirteen thousand feet above sea-level. The ptarmigan, with their home above tree-line, amid eternal snows, are wonderfully self-reliant and self-contained. The ouzel, too, is self-poised, indifferent to all the world but his brook,

PTARMIGAN

and showing an appreciation for water greater, I think, than that of any other landsman. These birds, the ptarmigan and the ouzel, along with the willow thrush, who sings out his melody amid the shadows of the pines, who puts his woods into song,—these birds of the mountains are with me when memory takes me back a solitary visitor to the lonely places of the Rockies.

The birds of the Rockies, as well as the bigger folk who live there, have ways of their own which distinguish them from their kind in the East. They sing with more enthusiasm, but with the same subtle tone that everywhere tells that all is right with the world, and makes all to the manner born glad to be alive.

Nothing delights me more than to come across a person who is interested in trees; and I have long thought that any one who appreciates trees or birds is one who is either good or great, or both. I consider it an honor to converse with one who knows the birds and the trees, and have more than once gone out of my way to meet one of those favored mortals. I remember one cold morning I came down off the mountains and went into a house to get warm. Rather I went in to scrape an acquaintance with whomsoever could be living there who remembered the birds while snow and cold prevailed, — when Nature forgot. To get warm was a palpable excuse. I was not cold; I had no need to stop; I simply wanted to meet the people who had, on this day at least, put out food and warm water for the birds; but I have ever since been glad that I went in, for the house shielded from the cold a family whom it is good to know, and, besides making their acquaintance, I met " Bob " and heard her story.

Every one in the house was fond of pets. Rex, a huge St. Bernard, greeted me at the door, and with a show of satisfaction accompanied me to a chair near the stove. In going to the chair some forlorn snowbirds, " that Sarah had found nearly frozen while out feeding the birds this morning," hopped out of my way. As I sat down, I noticed an old sack on the floor against the wall before me. All at once this sack came to life, had an idea, or was bewitched, I thought. Anyway it became so active that it held my attention for several seconds, and gave me a little alarm. I was relieved when out of it tumbled an aggressive rooster, which advanced a few steps, flapped, and crowed lustily. " He was brought in to get thawed out; I suppose you will next be wondering where we keep the pig," said my hostess as she advanced to stir the fire, after which she examined " two little cripples," birds in a box behind the stove.

I moved to a cooler seat, by a door which led into an adjoining room. After I had sat down, " Bob," a pet quail, came from somewhere, and advanced with the most serene and dignified air to greet me. After pausing to eye me for a moment, with a look of mingled curiosity and satisfaction, she went under my chair and squatted confidingly on the floor. Bob was the first pet quail I had ever seen, and my questions concerning her brought from my hostess the following story : —

" One day last fall a flock of quail became frightened, and in their excited flight one struck against a neighbor's window and was badly stunned. My husband, who chanced to be near at the time, picked up the injured one and brought it home. My three daughters, who at times had had pet horses, snakes, turtles, and rats, welcomed this shy little stranger and at once set about caring for her injuries. Just before " Bob " had fully recovered, there came a heavy fall of snow, which was followed by such a succession of storms that we concluded to keep her with us, provided she was willing to stay. We gave her the freedom of the house. For some time she was wild and shy; under a chair or the lounge she would scurry if any one approached her. Plainly, she did not feel welcome or safe in our house, and I gave up the idea of taming her. One day, however, we had lettuce for dinner, and while we were at the table Sarah, my eldest daughter, who has a gift for taming and handling wild creatures, declared that Bob should eat out of her hand before night. All that afternoon she tempted her with bits of lettuce, and when evening came, had succeeded so well that never after was Bob afraid of us. Whenever we sat down for a meal, Bob would come running and quietly go in turn to each with coaxing sounds and pleading looks, wanting to be fed. It was against the rules to feed her at meals, but first one, then another, would slip something to her under the table, trying at the same time to appear innocent. The girls have always maintained that their mother, who made the rule, was the first one to break it. No one could resist Bob's pretty, dainty, coaxing ways.

" She is particularly fond of pie-crust, and many a time I have found the edge picked off the pie I had intended for dinner. Bob never fails to find a pie, if one is left uncovered. I think it is the shortening in the pie-crust that gives it the delicious flavor, for lard she prefers above all of her many foods. She cares least of all for grain. My daughters say that Bob's fondness for graham gems accounts for the frequency of their recent appearances on our table.

" After trying many places, Bob at last found a roosting-place that suited her. This was in a leather collar-box on the bureau, where she could nestle up close to her own image in the mirror. Since discovering this place she has never failed to occupy it at night. She is intelligent, and in so many ways pleasing that we are greatly attached to her."

Here I had to leave Bob and her good friends behind; but some months afterward my hostess of that winter day told me the concluding chapters of Bob's life.

" Bob disliked to be handled; though pleasing and irresistibly winsome, she was not in the least affectionate, and always maintained a dignified, ladylike reserve. But with the appearance of spring she showed signs of lonesomeness. With none of her kind to love, she turned to Rex and on him lavished all of her affection. When Rex was admitted to the house of a morning, she ran to meet him with a joyful cackle, — an utterance she did not use on any other occasion, — and with soft cooing sounds she followed him about the house. If Rex appeared bored with her attentions and walked away, she followed after, and persisted in tones that were surely scolding until he would lie down. Whenever he lay with his huge head between his paws, she would nestle down close to his face and remain content so long as he was quiet. Sometimes when he was lying down she would climb slowly over him; at each step she would put her foot down daintily, and as each foot touched him there was a slight movement of her head and a look of satisfaction. These climbs usually ended by her scratching in the long hair of his tail, and then nestling down into it.

"One day I was surprised to see her kiss Rex. When I told my family of this, they laughed heartily and were unable to believe me. Later, we all witnessed this pretty sight many times. She seemed to prefer to kiss him when he was lying down, with his head raised a little above the floor. Finding him in this position, she would walk beside him, reach up and kiss his face again and again, all the time cooing softly to him.

"Toward spring Bob's feathers became dull and somewhat ragged, and with the warm days came our decision to let her go outside. She was delighted to scratch in the loose earth around the rosebushes, and eagerly fed on the insects she found there. Her plumage soon took on its natural trimness and freshness. She did not show any inclination to leave, and with Rex by her or near her, we felt that she was safe from cats, so we soon allowed her to remain out all day long.

"Passers-by often stopped to watch Bob and

165

Rex playing together. Sometimes he would go lumbering across the yard while she, plainly displeased at the fast pace, hurried after with an incessant scolding chatter as much as to say: 'Don't go so fast, old fellow. How do you expect me to keep up?' Sometimes, when Rex was lying down eating a bone, she would stand on one of his fore legs and quietly pick away at the bone.

"The girls frequently went out to call her, and did so by whistling 'Bob White.' She never failed to answer promptly, and her response sounded like *chee chos*, *chee chos*, which she uttered before hurrying to them.

"One summer morning I found her at the kitchen door waiting to be let out. I opened the door and watched her go tripping down the steps. When she started across the yard I cautioned her to 'be a little lady, and don't get too far away.' Rex was away that morning, and soon one of the girls went out to call her. Repeated calls brought no answer. We all started searching. We wondered if the cat had caught her, or if she had been lured away by the winning calls of her kind. Beneath a cherry tree near the kitchen door, just as Rex came home, we found her, bloody and dead. Rex, after pushing her body tenderly about with his nose, as if trying to help her to rise, looked up and appealed piteously to us. We buried her beneath the rosebush near which she and Rex had played."

Kinnikinick

Kinnikinick

THE kinnikinick is a plant pioneer. Often it is the first plant to make a settlement or establish a colony on a barren or burned-over area. It is hardy, and is able to make a start and thrive in places so inhospitable as to afford most plants not the slightest foothold. In such places the kinnikinick's activities make changes which alter conditions so beneficially that in a little while plants less hardy come to join the first settler. The pioneer work done by the kinnikinick on a barren and rocky realm has often resulted in the establishment of a flourishing forest there.

The kinnikinick, or *Arctostaphylos Uva-Ursi*, as the botanists name it, may be called a ground-loving vine. Though always attractive, it is in winter that it is at its best. Then its bright green leaves and red berries shine among the snow-flowers in a quiet way that is strikingly beautiful.

Since it is beautiful as well as useful, I had

long admired this ever-cheerful, ever-spreading vine before I appreciated the good though humble work it is constantly doing. I had often stopped to greet it, — the only green thing upon a rock ledge or a sandy stretch, — had walked over it in forest avenues beneath tall and stately pines, and had slept comfortably upon its spicy, elastic rugs, liking it from the first. But on one of my winter tramps I fell in love with this beautiful evergreen.

The day was a cold one, and the high, gusty wind was tossing and playing with the last snowfall. I had been snowshoeing through the forest, and had come out upon an unsheltered ridge that was a part of a barren area which repeated fires had changed from a forested condition to desert. The snow lay several feet deep in the woods, but as the gravelly distance before me was bare, I took off my snowshoes. I went walking, and at times blowing, along the bleak ridge, scarcely able to see through the snow-filled air. But during a lull the air cleared of snow-dust and I paused to look about me. The wind still roared in the distance, and against the blue eastern sky it had a column of snow whirling that was dazzling white in the afternoon sun. On my left a mountain rose with easy slope to crag-crowned heights, and for miles swept away before me with seared side barren and dull. A few cloud-lets of snowdrifts and a scattering of mere tufts of snow stood out distinctly on this big, bare slope.

I wondered what could be holding these few spots of snow on this wind-swept slope. I finally went up to examine one of them. Thrust out and lifted just above the snow of the tuft before me was the jeweled hand of a kinnikinick; and every snow-deposit on the slope was held in place by the green arms of this plant. Here was this beau-tiful vinelike shrub gladly growing on a slope that had been forsaken by all other plants.

To state the situation fairly, all had been burned off by fire and Kinnikinick was the first to come back, and so completely had fires consumed the plant-food that many plants would be unable to live here until better conditions prevailed and the struggle for existence was made less severe. Kin-nikinick was making the needed changes; in time it would prepare the way, and other plants, and the pines too, would come back to carpet and plume the slope and prevent wind and water from tearing and scarring the earth.

The seeds of Kinnikinick are scattered by birds, chipmunks, wind, and water. I do not know by what agency the seeds had come to this slope, but here were the plants, and on this dry, fire-ruined, sun-scorched, wind-beaten slope they must have endured many hardships. Many must have perished before these living ones had made a secure start in life.

Once Kinnikinick has made a start, it is constantly assisted to succeed by its own growing success. Its arms catch and hold snow, and this gives a supply of much-needed water. This water is snugly stored beneath the plant, where but little can be reached or taken by the sun or the thirsty winds. The winds, too, which were so unfriendly while it was trying to make a start, now become helpful to the brave, persistent plant. Every wind that blows brings something to it, — dust, powdered earth, trash, the remains of dead insects; some of this material is carried for miles.

Kinnikinick

All goes to form new soil, or to fertilize or mulch the old. This supplies Kinnikinick's great needs. The plant grows rich from the constant tribute of the winds. The soil-bed grows deeper and richer and is also constantly outbuilding and enlarging, and Kinnikinick steadily increases its size.

In a few years a small oasis is formed in, or rather on, the barren. This becomes a place of refuge for seed wanderers, — in fact, a nursery. Up the slope I saw a young pine standing in a kinnikinick snow-cover. In the edge of the snow-tuft by me, covered with a robe of snow, I found a tiny tree, a mere baby pine. Where did this pine come from? There were no seed-bearing pines within miles. How did a pine seed find its way to this cosy nursery? Perhaps the following is its story: The seed of this little pine, together with a score or more of others, grew in a cone out near the end of the pine-tree limb. This pine was on a mountain several miles from the fire-ruined slope, when one windy autumn day some time after the seeds were ripe, the cone began to open its fingers and the seeds came dropping out.

The seed of this baby tree was one of these, and when it tumbled out of the cone the wind caught it, and away it went over trees, rocks, and gulches, whirling and dancing in the autumn sunlight. After tumbling a few miles in this wild flight, it came down among some boulders. Here it lay until, one very windy day, it was caught up and whirled away again. Before long it was dashed against a granite cliff and fell to the ground; but in a moment, the wind found it and drove it, with a shower of trash and dust, bounding and leaping across a barren slope, plump into this kinnikinick nest. From this shelter the wind could not drive it. Here the little seed might have said, "This is just the place I was looking for; here is shelter from the wind and sun; the soil is rich and damp; I am so tired, I think I'll take a sleep." When the little seed awoke, it wore the green dress of the pine family. The kinnikinick's nursery had given it a start in life.

Under favorable conditions Kinnikinick is a comparatively rapid grower. Its numerous vine-like limbs—little arms—spread or reach outward from the central root, take a new hold upon the earth, and prepare to reach again. The ground beneath it in a little while is completely hidden by its closely crowding leafy arms. In places these soft, pliable rugs unite and form extensive carpets. Strip off these carpets and often all that remains is a barren exposure of sand or gravel on bald or broken rocks, whose surfaces and edges have been draped or buried by its green leaves and red berries.

In May kinnikinick rugs become flower-beds. Each flower is a narrow-throated, pink-lipped, creamy-white jug, and is filled with a drop of exquisitely flavored honey. The jugs in a short time change to smooth purple berries, and in autumn they take on their winter dress of scarlet. When ripe the berries taste like mealy crab-apples. I have often seen chipmunks eating the berries, or apples, sitting up with the fruit in both their deft little hands, and eating it with such evident relish that I frequently found myself thinking of these berries as chipmunk's apples.

Kinnikinick is widely distributed over the earth, and is most often found on gravelly slopes or sandy stretches. Frequently you will find it among scattered pines, trying to carpet their cathedral floor. Many a summer day I have lain down and rested on these flat and fluffy forest rugs, while between the tangled tops of the pines I looked at the blue of the sky or watched the white clouds so serenely floating there. Many a summer night upon these elastic spreads I have lain and gazed at the thick-sown stars, or watched the ebbing, fading camp-fire, at last to fall asleep and to rest as sweetly and serenely as ever did the Scotchman upon his heathered Highlands. Many a morning I have awakened late after a sleep so long that I had settled into the yielding mass and Kinnikinick had put up an arm, either to shield my face with its hand, or to show me, when I should awaken, its pretty red berries and bright green leaves.

One morning, while visiting in a Blackfoot Indian camp, I saw the men smoking kinnikinick leaves, and I asked if they had any legend concerning the shrub. I felt sure they must have a fascinating story of it which told of the Great Spirit's love for Kinnikinick, but they had none. One of them said he had heard the Piute Indians tell

SUMMER AT AN ALTITUDE OF 12,000 FEET

Kinnikinick

why the Great Spirit had made it, but he could
not remember the account. I inquired among
many Indians, feeling that I should at last learn
a happy legend concerning it, but in vain. One
night, however, by my camp-fire, I dreamed that
some Alaska Indians told me this legend: —

Long, long ago, Kinnikinick was a small tree
with brown berries and broad leaves which
dropped to the ground in autumn. One year a
great snow came while the leaves were still on,
and all trees were flattened upon the ground by
the weight of the clinging snow. All broad-leaved
trees except Kinnikinick died. When the snow
melted, Kinnikinick was still alive, but pressed
out upon the ground, crushed so that it could not
rise. It started to grow, however, and spread out
its limbs on the surface very like a root growth.
The Great Spirit was so pleased with Kinnikinick's efforts that he decided to let it live on in
its new form, and also that he would send it to
colonize many places where it had never been.
He changed its berries from brown to red, so
that the birds could see its fruit and scatter its
seeds far and wide. Its leaves were reduced in

size and made permanently green, so that Kinnikinick, like the pines it loves and helps, could wear green all the time.

Whenever I see a place that has been made barren and ugly by the thoughtlessness of man, I like to think of Kinnikinick, for I know it will beautify these places if given a chance to do so. There are on earth millions of acres now almost desert that may some time be changed and beautified by this cheerful, modest plant. Some time many bald and barren places in the Rockies will be plumed with pines, bannered with flowers, have brooks, butterflies, and singing birds, — all of these, and homes, too, around which children will play, — because of the reclaiming work which will be done by charming Kinnikinick.

The Lodge-Pole Pine

The Lodge-Pole Pine

THE trappers gave the Lodge-Pole Pine (*Pinus contorta*, var. *Murrayana*) its popular name on account of its general use by Indians of the West for lodge or wigwam poles. It is a tree with an unusually interesting life-story, and is worth knowing for the triumphant struggle which it makes for existence, and also for the commercial importance which, at an early date, it seems destined to have. Perhaps its most interesting and advantageous characteristic is its habit of holding or hoarding its seed-harvests.

Lodge-pole is also variously called Tamarack, Murray, and Two-leaved Pine. Its yellow-green needles are in twos, and are from one to three inches in length. Its cones are about one inch in diameter at the base and from one to two inches long. Its light-gray or cinnamon-gray bark is thin and scaly.

In a typical lodge-pole forest the trees, or poles, stand closely together and all are of the same age and of even size. Seedlings and saplings are not seen in an old forest. This forest covers the mountains for miles, growing in moist, dry, and stony places, claims all slopes, has an altitudinal range of four thousand feet, and almost entirely excludes all other species from its borders.

The hoarding habit of this tree, the service rendered it by forest fires, the lightness of the seeds and the readiness with which they germinate on dry or burned-over areas, its ability to grow in a variety of soils and climates, together with its capacity to thrive in the full glare of the sun, — all these are factors which make this tree interesting, and which enable it, despite the most dangerous forest enemy, fire, to increase and multiply and extend its domains.

During the last fifty years this aggressive, indomitable tree has enormously extended its area, and John Muir is of the opinion that, "as fires are multiplied and the mountains become drier, this wonderful lodge-pole pine bids fair to obtain possession of nearly all the forest ground in the West." Its geographical range is along the Rocky Mountains from Alaska to New Mexico, and on

A TYPICAL LODGE-POLE FOREST

the Pacific coast forests of it are, in places, found from sea-level to an altitude of eleven thousand feet. On the Rockies it flourishes between the altitudes of seven thousand and ten thousand feet. It is largely represented in the forests of Colorado, Utah, Idaho, and Montana, and it has extensive areas in Oregon and Washington. It is the most numerous tree in Wyoming, occupying in Yellowstone Park a larger area than all other trees combined, while in California it forms the bulk of the alpine forests.

The lodge-pole readily adapts itself to the most diverse soil and conditions, but it thrives best where there is considerable moisture. The roots accommodate themselves to shallow soil, and thrive in it.

This tree begins to bear fruit at an early age, sometimes when only eight years old, and usually produces large quantities of cones annually. The cones sometimes open and liberate the seeds as soon as they are ripe, but commonly they remain on the tree for years, with their seeds carefully sealed and protected beneath the scales. So far as I have observed, the trees on the driest soil cling longest to their seeds. For an old lodge-pole to have on its limbs twenty crops of un-opened cones is not uncommon. Neither is it uncommon to see an extensive lodge-pole forest each tree of which has upon it several hundred, and many of the trees a few thousand, cones, and in each cone a few mature seeds. Most of these seeds will never have a chance to make a start in life except they be liberated by fire. In fact, most lodge-pole seeds are liberated by fire. The reproduction of this pine is so interwoven with the effects of the forest fires that one may safely say that most of the lodge-pole forests and the increasing lodge-pole areas are the result of forest fires.

Every lodge-pole forest is a fire-trap. The thin, scaly, pitchy bark and the live resiny needles on the tree, as well as those on the ground, are very inflammable, and fires probably sweep a lodge-pole forest more frequently than any other in America. When this forest is in a sapling stage, it is very likely to be burned to ashes. If, how-ever, the trees are beyond the sapling stage, the fire probably will consume the needles, burn some of the bark away, and leave the tree, together with its numerous seed-filled cones, unconsumed. As a rule, the fire so heats the cones that most of them open and release their seeds a few hours, or a few days, after the fire. If the area burned over is a large one, the fire loosens the clasp of the cone-scales and millions of lodge-pole seeds are released to be sown by the great eternal seed-sower, the wind. These seeds are thickly scattered, and as they germinate readily in the mineral soil, enormous numbers of them sprout and begin to struggle for existence. I once counted 84,322 young trees on an acre.

The trees often stand as thick as wheat in a field and exclude all other species. Their growth is slow and mostly upright. They early become delicate miniature poles, and often, at the age of twenty-five or thirty years, good fishing-poles. In their crowded condition, the competition is deadly. Hundreds annually perish, but this tree clings tenaciously to life, and starving it to death is not easy. In the summer of 1895 I counted 24,271 thirty-year-old lodge-poles upon an acre. Ten years later, 19,040 of these were alive. It is possible that eighty thousand, or even one hundred thousand, seedlings started upon this acre. Sometimes more than half a century is required for the making of good poles.

On the Grand River in Colorado I once measured a number of poles that averaged two inches in diameter at the ground and one and one half inches fifteen feet above it. These poles averaged forty feet high and were sixty-seven years of age. Others of my notes read: "9728 trees upon an acre. They were one hundred and three years of age, two to six inches in diameter, four and a half feet from the ground, and from thirty to sixty feet high, at an altitude of 8700 feet. Soil and moisture conditions were excellent. On another acre there were 4126 trees one hundred and fifty-four years old, together with eleven young Engelmann spruces and one *Pinus flexilis* and eight Douglas firs. The accumulation of duff, mostly needles, averaged eight inches deep, and, with the exception of one bunch of kinnikinick, there was neither grass nor weed, and only tiny, thinly scattered sun-gold reached the brown matted floor."

The Lodge-Pole Pine

After self-thinning has gone on for a hundred years or so, the ranks have been so thinned that there are openings sufficiently large to allow other species a chance to come in. By this time, too, there is sufficient humus on the floor to allow the seeds of many other species to germinate. Lodge-pole thus colonizes barren places, holds them for a time, and so changes them that the very species dispossessed by fire may regain the lost territory. Roughly, the lodge-pole will hold the ground exclusively from seventy-five to one hundred and fifty years, then the invading trees will come triumphantly in and, during the next century and a half, will so increase and multiply that they will almost exclude the lodge-pole. Thus Engelmann spruce and Douglas fir are now growing where lodge-pole flourished, but let fire destroy this forest and lodge-pole will again claim the territory, hold it against all comers for a century or two, and then slowly give way to or be displaced by the spruces and firs.

The interesting characteristic of holding its cones and hoarding seeds often results in the cones being overgrown and embedded in the trunk or the limbs of the trees. As the cones hug closely the trunk or the limbs, it is not uncommon for the saw, when laying open a log at the mill, to reveal a number of cones embedded there. I have in my cabin a sixteen-foot plank that is two inches in diameter and six inches wide, which came out of a lodge-pole tree. Embedded in this are more than a score of cones. Probably most of these cones were of the first crop which the tree produced, for they clung along the trunk of the tree and grew there when it was about an inch and a quarter in diameter. The section upon which these cones grew was between fifteen and twenty-five feet from the ground.

The seeds of most conifers need vegetable mould, litter, or vegetation cover of some kind in which to germinate, and then shade for a time in which to grow. These requirements so needed by other conifer seeds and seedlings are detrimental to the lodge-pole. If its seeds fall on areas lightly covered with low huckleberry vines, but few of them will germinate. A lodge-pole seed that germinates in the shade is doomed. It must have sunlight or die. In the ashes of a forest fire, in the full glare of the sun, the seeds of the lodge-pole germinate, grow, and flourish.

Wind is the chief agency which enables the seeds to migrate. The seeds are light, and I know of one instance where an isolated tree on a plateau managed to scatter its seeds by the aid of the wind over a circular area fifty acres in extent, though a few acres is all that is reached by the average tree. Sometimes the wind scatters the seeds unevenly. If most of the seeds are released in one day, and the wind this day prevails from the same quarter, the seeds will take but one course from the tree; while changing winds may scatter them quite evenly all around the tree.

A camping party built a fire against a lone lodge-pole. The tree was killed and suffered a loss of its needles from the fire. Four years later, a long green pennant, tattered at the end and formed of lodge-pole seedlings, showed on the mountain-side. This pennant began at the tree and streamed out more than seven hundred feet. Its width varied from ten to fifty feet.

The action of a fire in a lodge-pole forest is varied. If the forest be an old one, even with much rubbish on the ground the heat is not so intense as in a young growth. Where trees are scattered the flames crawl from tree to tree, the needles of which ignite like flash-powder and make beautiful rose-purple flames. At night fires of this kind furnish rare fireworks. Each tree makes a fountain of flame, after which, for a moment, every needle shines like incandescent silver, while exquisite light columns of ashen green smoke float above. The hottest fire I ever experienced was made by the burning of a thirty-eight-year lodge-pole forest. In this forest the poles stood more than thirty feet high, and were about fifteen thousand to an acre. They stood among masses of fallen trees, the remains of a spruce forest that had been killed by the same fire which had given this lodge-pole forest a chance to spring up. Several thousand acres were burned, and for a brief time the fire traveled swiftly. I saw it roll blazing over one mountain-side at a speed of more than sixty miles an hour. It was intensely hot, and in a surprisingly short time the flames had burned every log, stump, and tree to ashes. Several hundred acres were swept absolutely bare of trees, living and dead, and the roots too were burned far into the ground.

Several beetles prey upon the lodge-pole, and in some localities the porcupine feeds off its inner bark. It is also made use of by man. The wood is light, not strong, with a straight, rather coarse grain. It is of a light yellow to nearly white, or pinkish white, soft, and easily worked. In the West it is extensively used for lumber, fencing, fuel, and log houses, and millions of lodge-pole railroad-ties are annually put to use.

Most lodge-poles grow in crowded ranks, and slow growth is the result, but it is naturally a comparatively rapid grower. In good, moist soil, uncrowded, it rapidly builds upward and outward. I have more than a score of records that show that it has made a quarter of an inch diameter growth annually, together with an upright growth of more than twelve inches, and also several notes which show where trees standing in favorable conditions have made half an inch diameter growth annually. This fact of its rapid growth, together with other valuable characteristics and qualities of the tree, may lead it to be selected by the government for the reforestation of millions of acres of denuded areas in the West. In many places on the Rockies it would, if given a chance, make commercial timber in from thirty to sixty years.

I examined a lodge-pole in the Medicine Bow Mountains that was scarred by fire. It was two hundred and fourteen years of age. It took one hundred and seventy-eight years for it to make five inches of diameter growth. In the one hundred and seventy-eighth ring of annual growth there was a fire-scar, and during the next thirty-six years it put on five more inches of growth. It is probable, therefore, that the fire destroyed the neighboring trees, which had dwarfed and starved it and thus held it in check. I know of scores of cases where lodge-poles grew much more rapidly, though badly fire-scarred, after fires had removed their hampering competitors.

There are millions of acres of young lodge-pole forests in the West. They are almost as impenetrable as canebrakes. It would greatly increase the rate of growth if these trees were thinned, but it is probable that this will not be done for many years. Meantime, if these forests be pro-

tected from fire, they will be excellent water-con-
servers. When the snows or the rains fall into
the lodge-pole thickets, they are beyond the reach
of the extra dry winds. If they are protected, the
water-supply of the West will be protected; and
if they are destroyed, the winds will evaporate
most of the precipitation that falls upon their
areas.

I do not know of any tree that better adjusts
itself to circumstances, or that struggles more
bravely or successfully. I am hopeful that before
many years the school-children of America will
be well acquainted with the Lodge-Pole Pine, and
I feel that its interesting ways, its struggles, and
its importance will, before long, be appreciated
and win a larger place in our literature and also
in our hearts.

Rocky Mountain Forests

Rocky Mountain Forests

IT is stirring to stand at the feet of the Rocky Mountains and look upward and far away over the broken strata that pile and terrace higher and higher, until, at a distance of twenty-five or thirty miles, they stand a shattered and snowy horizon against the blue. The view is an inspiring one from the base, but it gives no idea that this mountain array is a magnificent wild hanging-garden. Across the terraced and verdure-plumed garden the eternal snows send their clear and constant streams, to leap in white cascades between crowning crags and pines. Upon the upper slopes of this garden are many mirrored lakes, ferny, flowery glens, purple forests, and crag-piled meadows.

If any one were to start at the foothills in Colorado, where one of the clear streams comes sweeping out of the mountains to go quietly across the wide, wide plains, and from this starting-place climb to the crest of this terraced land of crags, pines, ferns, and flowers, he would, in so doing, go through many life-zones and see numerous standing and moving life-forms, all struggling, yet seemingly all contented with life and the scenes wherein they live and struggle.

The broad-leaf cottonwood, which has accompanied the streams across the plains, stops at the foothills, and along the river in the foothills the narrow-leaf cottonwood (*Populus angustifolia*) crowds the water's edge, here and there mingling with red-fruited hawthorns and wild plums (*Prunus Americana*). A short distance from the stream the sumac stands brilliant in the autumn, and a little farther away are clumps of greasewood and sagebrush and an occasional spread of juniper. Here and there are some forlorn-looking red cedars and a widely scattered sprinkling of stunted yellow pines (*Pinus scopulorum*).

At an altitude of six thousand feet the yellow pine acquires true tree dignity and begins to mass itself into forests. When seen from a distance its appearance suggests the oak. It seems a trifle rigid, appears ready to meet emergencies, has a look of the heroic, and carries more character than any other tree on the Rockies. Though a slender and small-limbed tree in youth, after forty or fifty years it changes slowly and becomes stocky, strong-limbed, and rounded at the top. Lightning, wind, and snow break or distort its upper limbs so that most of these veteran pines show a picturesquely broken top, with a towering dead limb or two among the green ones. Its needles are in bundles of both twos and threes, and they vary from three to eight inches in length. The tree is rich in resin, and a walk through its groves on an autumn day, when the sun shines bright on its clean golden columns and brings out its aroma, is a walk full of contentment and charm. The bark is fluted and blackish-gray in youth, and it breaks up into irregular plates, which on old trees frequently are five inches or more in thickness. This bark gives the tree excellent fire-protection.

The yellow pine is one of the best fire-fighters and lives long. I have seen many of the pines that were from sixty to ninety feet high, with a diameter of from three to five feet. They were aged from two hundred and fifty to six hundred years. Most of the old ones have lived through several fires. I dissected a fallen veteran that grew on the St. Vrain watershed, at an altitude of eight thousand feet, that was eight-five feet high and fifty-one inches in diameter five feet from the ground. It showed six hundred and seventy-nine annual rings. During the first three hundred years of its life it averaged an inch of diameter growth every ten years. It had been through many forest fires and showed large fire-scars. One of these it received at the age of three hundred and thirty-nine years. It carried another scar which it received two hundred and sixteen years before its death; another which it received in 1830; and a fourth which it received fourteen years before it blew over in the autumn of 1892. All of these fire-scars were on the same quarter of the tree. All were on that part of the tree which overlooked the down-sloping hillside.

Forest fires, where there is opportunity, sweep up the mountain-side against the lower side of the trees. The lower side is thus often scarred while the opposite side is scarcely injured; but wind blowing down the gulch at the time of each fire may have directed the flames against the lower side of this tree. In many places clusters of young trees were growing close to the lower side of the old trees, and were enabled to grow there by light that came in from the side. It may be that the heat from one of the blazing clusters scarred this old pine; then another young cluster may have grown, to be in time also consumed. But these scars may have resulted, wholly or in part, from other causes.

Yellow pine claims the major portion of the well-drained slopes, except those that are northerly, in the middle mountain-zone up to the lower lodge-pole margin. A few groves are found higher than nine thousand feet. Douglas spruce covers many of the northerly slopes that lie between six thousand and nine thousand feet.

The regularity of tree-distribution over the mountains is to me a never-failing source of interest. Though the various species of trees appear to be growing almost at random, yet each species shows a decided preference for peculiar altitude, soil, temperature, and moisture conditions. It is an interesting demonstration of tree adaptability to follow a stream which comes out of the west, in the middle mountain-zone, and observe how unlike the trees are which thrive on opposite sides. On the southerly slopes that come down to the water is an open forest of yellow pine, and on the opposite side, the south bank, a dense forest of Douglas spruce. If one be told the altitude, the slope, and the moisture conditions of a place on the Rockies, he should, if acquainted with the Rockies, be able to name the kinds of trees growing there. Some trees grow only in moist places, others only in dry places, some never below or above a certain altitude. Indeed, so regular is the tree-distribution over the Rockies that I feel certain, if I were to awaken from a Rip Van Winkle sleep in the forests on the middle or upper slopes of these mountains, I could, after examining a few of the trees around me, tell the points of the compass, the altitude above sea-level, and the season of the year.

At an altitude of about sixty-five hundred feet cottonwood, which has accompanied the streams from the foothills, begins to be displaced by aspen. The aspen (*Populus tremuloides*) is found growing in groups and groves from this altitude

ASPENS

up to timber-line, usually in the moister places. To me the aspen is almost a classic tree, and I have met it in so many places that I regard it almost as an old friend. It probably rivals the juniper in being the most widely distributed tree on the North American continent. It also vies with the lodge-pole pine in quickness of taking possession of burned-over areas. Let a moist place be burned over and the aspen will quickly take possession, and soon establish conditions which will allow conifers to return. This the conifers do, and in a very short time smother the aspens that made it possible for them to start in life. The good nursery work of aspens is restricted pretty closely to damp places.

Besides being a useful tree, the bare-legged little aspen with its restless and childlike ways is a tree that it is good to know. When alone, these little trees seem lonely and sometimes to tremble- as though just a little afraid in this big strange world. But generally the aspen is not alone. Usually you find a number of little aspens playing together, with their leaves shaking, jostling, and jumping, — moving all the time. If you go near a group and stop to watch them, they may, for an instant, pause to glance at you, then turn to romp more merrily than before. And they have other childlike ways besides bare legs and activity. On some summer day, if you wish to find these little trees, look for them where you would for your own child, — wading the muddiest place to be found. They like to play in the swamps, and may often be seen in a line alongside a brook with toes in the water, as though looking for the deepest place before wading in.

One day I came across a party of merry little aspens who were in a circle around a grand old pine, as though using the pine for a maypole to dance around. It was in autumn, and each little aspen wore its gayest colors. Some were in gowns of new-made cloth-of-gold. The grizzled old pine, like an old man in the autumn of his life, looked down as though honored and pleased with the happy little ones who seemed so full of joy. I watched them for a time and went on across the mountains; but I have long believed in fairies, so the next day I went back to see this fairyland and found the dear little aspens still shaking their golden leaves, while the old pine stood still in the sunlight.

Along the streams, between the altitudes of sixty-five hundred and eighty-five hundred feet, one finds the Colorado blue or silver spruce. This tree grows in twos or threes, occasionally forming a small grove. Usually it is found growing near a river or brook, standing closely to a golden-lichened crag, in surroundings which emphasize its beauty of form and color. With its fluffy silver-tipped robe and its garlands of cones it is the handsomest tree on the Rockies. It is the queen of these wild gardens. Beginning at the altitude where the silver spruce ceases is the beautiful balsam fir (*Abies lasiocarpa*). The balsam fir is generally found in company with the alders or the silver spruce near a brook. It is strikingly symmetrical and often forms a perfect slender cone. The balsam fir and the silver spruce are the evergreen poems of the wild. They get into one's heart like the hollyhock. Several years ago the school-children of Colorado selected by vote a State flower and a State tree. Although more than fifty flowers received votes, two thirds of all the votes went to the Rocky Mountain columbine. When it came to selecting a tree, every vote was cast for the silver spruce.

Edwinia, with its attractive waxy white flowers, and potentilla, with bloom of gold, are shrubs which lend a charm to much of the mountain-section. Black birch and alder trim many of the streams, and the mountain maple is thinly scattered from the foothills to nine thousand feet altitude. Wild roses are frequently found near the maple, and gooseberry bushes fringe many a brook. Huckleberries flourish on the timbered slopes, and kinnikinick gladdens many a gravelly stretch or slope.

Between the altitudes of eight thousand and ten thousand feet there are extensive forests of the indomitable lodge-pole pine. This borders even more extensive forests of Engelmann spruce. Lodge-pole touches timber-line in a few places, and Engelmann spruce climbs up to it in every cañon or moist depression. Along with these, at timber-line, are *flexilis* pine, balsam fir, arctic willow, dwarf black birch, and the restless little aspen. All timber-line trees are dwarfed and most

A GROVE OF SILVER SPRUCE

of them distorted. Conditions at timber-line are severe, but the presence, in places, of young trees farthest up the slopes suggests that these severe conditions may be developing hardier trees than any that now are growing on this forest frontier. If this be true, then timber-line on the Rockies is yet to gain a higher limit.

Since the day of "Pike's Peak or bust," fires have swept over more than half of the primeval forest area in Colorado. Some years ago, while making special efforts to prevent forest fires from starting, I endeavored to find out the cause of these fires. I regretfully found that most of them were the result of carelessness, and I also made a note to the effect that there are few worse things to be guilty of than carelessly setting fire to a forest. Most of these forest fires had their origin from camp-fires which the departing campers had left unextinguished. There were sixteen fires in one summer, which I attributed to the following causes: campers, nine; cigar, one; lightning, one; locomotive, one; stockmen, two; sheep-herders, one; and sawmill, one.

Fires have made the Rocky Mountains still

more rocky. In many places the fires burn their way to solid rock. In other places the humus, or vegetable mould, is partly consumed by fire, and the remainder is in a short time blown away by wind or washed away by water. Fires often leave only blackened granite rock behind, so that in many places they have not only consumed the forests, but also the food upon which the new forests might have fed. Many areas where splendid forests grew, after being fire-swept, show only barren granite. As some of the granite on the Rockies disintegrates slowly, it will probably require several hundred years for Nature to resoil and reforest some of these fire-scarred places. However, upon thousands of acres of the Rockies millions of young trees are just beginning to grow, and if these trees be protected from fire, a forest will early result.

I never see a little tree bursting from the earth, peeping confidently up among the withered leaves, without wondering how long it will live or what trials or triumphs it will have. I always hope that it will find life worth living, and that it will live long to better and to beautify the earth. I hope it will love the blue sky and the white clouds passing by. I trust it will welcome all seasons and ever join merrily in the music, the motion, and the movement of the elemental dance with the winds. I hope it will live with rapture in the flower-opening days of spring and also enjoy the quiet summer rain. I hope it will be a home for the birds and hear their low, sweet mating-songs. I trust that when comes the golden peace of autumn days, it will be ready with fruited boughs for the life to come. I never fail to hope that if this tree is cut down, it may be used for a flag-pole to keep our glorious banner in the blue above, or that it may be built into a cottage where love will abide; or if it must be burnt, that it will blaze on the hearthstone in a home where children play in the firelight on the floor.

In many places the Rockies rise more than three thousand feet above the heights where live the highest struggling trees at timber-line, but these steep alpine slopes are not bare. The rocks are tinted with lichens. In places are miles of grassy slopes and miniature meadows, covered with coarse sedges and bright tender flowers. Among the shrubs the *Betula glandulosa* is probably commonest, while *Dasiphora fruticosa* and *Salix chlorophylla* are next in prominence. Here and there you will see the golden gaillardia, the silver and blue columbines, splendid arrays of sedum, many marsh-marigolds, lungworts, paint-brushes of red and white and yellow green, beds of purple primroses, sprinklings of alpine gentians, many clusters of live-forever, bunches of honey-smelling valerian, with here and there standing the tall stalks of fraseria, or monument-plant. There are hundreds of other varieties of plants, and the region above timber-line holds many treasures that are dear to those who love flowers and who appreciate them especially where cold and snow keep them tiny.

Above timber-line are many bright blossoms that are familiar to us, but dwarfed to small size. One needs to get down and lie upon the ground and search carefully with a magnifying-glass, or he will overlook many of these brave bright but tiny flowers. Here are blue gentians less than half an inch in height, bell-flowers only a trifle higher, and alpine willows so tiny that their catkins touch the ground. One of the most attractive and beautiful of these alpine flowers is the blue honeysuckle or polemonium, about an inch in height. I have found it on mountain-tops, in its fresh, clear coloring, at an altitude of fourteen thousand feet, as serene as the sky above it.

A climb up the Rockies will develop a love for nature, strengthen one's appreciation of the beautiful world outdoors, and put one in tune with the Infinite. It will inspire one with the feeling that the Rockies have a rare mountain wealth of their own. They are not to be compared with the Selkirks or the Alps or any other unlike range of mountains. The Rockies are not a type, but an individuality, singularly rich in mountain scenes which stir one's blood and which strengthen and sweeten life.

Besieged by Bears

Besieged by Bears

Two old prospectors, Sullivan and Jason, once took me in for the night, and after supper they related a number of interesting experiences. Among these tales was one of the best bear-stories I have ever heard. The story was told in the graphic, earnest, realistic style so often possessed by those who have lived strong, stirring lives among crags and pines. Although twenty years had gone by, these prospectors still had a vivid recollection of that lively night when they were besieged by three bears, and in recounting the experience they mingled many good word-pictures of bear behavior with their exciting and amusing story. " This happened to us," said Sullivan, " in spite of the fact that we were minding our own business and had never hunted bears."

The siege occurred at their log cabin during the spring of 1884. They were prospecting in Geneva Park, where they had been all winter, driving a tunnel. They were so nearly out of supplies that they could not wait for snowdrifts to melt out of the trail. Provisions must be had, and Sullivan thought that, by allowing twice the usual time, he could make his way down through the drifts and get back to the cabin with them. So one morning, after telling Jason that he would be back the next evening, he took their burro and set off down the mountain. On the way home next day Sullivan had much difficulty in getting the loaded burro through the snowdrifts, and when within a mile of the cabin, they stuck fast. Sullivan unpacked and rolled the burro out of the snow, and was busily repacking, when the animal's uneasiness made him look round.

In the edge of the woods, only a short distance away, were three bears, apparently a mother and her two well-grown children. They were sniffing the air eagerly and appeared somewhat excited. The old bear would rise on her hind paws, sniff the air, then drop back to the ground. She kept her nose pointed toward Sullivan, but did not appear to look at him. The smaller bears moved restlessly about; they would walk a few steps in advance, stand erect, draw their fore paws close

OURAY, COLORADO

A typical mining town

to their breasts, and sniff, sniff, sniff the air, upward and in all directions before them. Then
they would slowly back up to the old bear. They
all seemed very good-natured.

When Sullivan was unpacking the burro, the
wrapping had come off two hams which were
among the supplies, and the wind had carried the
delicious aroma to the bears, who were just out
of their winter dens after weeks of fasting. Of
course, sugar-cured hams smelled good to them.
Sullivan repacked the burro and went on. The
bears quietly eyed him for some distance. At a
turn in the trail he looked back and saw the bears
clawing and smelling the snow on which the provisions had lain while he was getting the burro
out of the snowdrift. He went on to the cabin,
had supper, and forgot the bears.

The log cabin in which he and Jason lived was
a small one; it had a door in the side and a small
window in one end. The roof was made of a
layer of poles thickly covered with earth. A large
shepherd-dog often shared the cabin with the
prospectors. He was a playful fellow, and Sullivan often romped with him. Near their cabin were

some vacant cabins of other prospectors, who had " gone out for the winter " and were not yet back for summer prospecting.

The evening was mild, and as soon as supper was over Sullivan filled his pipe, opened the door, and sat down on the edge of the bed for a smoke, while Jason washed the dishes. He had taken only a few pulls at his pipe when there was a rattling at the window. Thinking the dog was outside, Sullivan called, " Why don't you go round to the door ? " This invitation was followed by a momentary silence, then smash ! a piece of sash and fragments of window-glass flew past Sullivan and rattled on the floor. He jumped to his feet. In the dim candle-light he saw a bear's head coming in through the window. He threw his pipe of burning tobacco into the bear's face and eyes, and then grabbed for some steel drills which lay in the corner on the floor. The earth roof had leaked, and the drills were ice-covered and frozen fast to the floor.

While Sullivan was dislodging the drills, Jason began to bombard the bear vigorously with plates from the table. The bear backed out; she was looking for food, not clean plates. However, the instant she was outside, she accepted Sullivan's invitation and went round to the door! And she came for it with a rush! Both Sullivan and Jason jumped to close the door. They were not quick enough, and instead of one bear there were three! The entire family had accepted the invitation, and all were trying to come in at once!

When Sullivan and Jason threw their weight against the door it slammed against the big bear's nose, — a very sensitive spot. She gave a savage growl. Apparently she blamed the two other bears either for hurting her nose or for being in the way. At any rate, a row started; halfway in the door the bears began to fight; for a few seconds it seemed as if all the bears would roll inside. Sullivan and Jason pushed against the door with all their might, trying to close it. During the struggle the bears rolled outside and the door went shut with a bang. The heavy securing cross-bar was quickly put into place; but not a moment too soon, for an instant later the old bear gave a furious growl and flung herself against the door, making it fairly crack; it seemed as if the door would be broken in. Sullivan and Jason hurriedly knocked their slab bed to pieces and used the slats and heavy sides to prop and strengthen the door. The bears kept surging and clawing at the door, and while the prospectors were spiking the braces against it and giving their entire attention to it, they suddenly felt the cabin shake and heard the logs strain and give. They started back, to see the big bear struggling in the window. Only the smallness of the window had prevented the bear from getting in unnoticed, and surprising them while they were bracing the door. The window was so small that the bear in trying to get in had almost wedged fast. With hind paws on the ground, fore paws on the window-sill, and shoulders against the log over the window, the big bear was in a position to exert all her enormous strength. Her efforts to get in sprung the logs and gave the cabin the shake which warned.

Sullivan grabbed one of the steel drills and dealt the bear a terrible blow on the head. She gave a growl of mingled pain and fury as she freed herself from the window. Outside she backed off growling.

Besieged by Bears

For a little while things were calmer. Sullivan
and Jason, drills in hand, stood guard at the window. After some snarling in front of the window
the bears went round to the door. They clawed
the door a few times and then began to dig under
it. " They are tunneling in for us," said Sullivan.
"They want those hams; but they won't get
them."

After a time the bears quit digging and started
away, occasionally stopping to look hesitatingly
back. It was almost eleven o'clock, and the full
moon shone splendidly through the pines. The
prospectors hoped that the bears were gone for
good. There was an old rifle in the cabin, but
there were no cartridges, for Sullivan and Jason
never hunted and rarely had occasion to fire a
gun. But, fearing that the animals might return,
Sullivan concluded to go to one of the vacant
cabins for a loaded Winchester which he knew
to be there.

As soon as the bears disappeared, he crawled
out of the window and looked cautiously around;
then he made a run for the vacant cabin. The
bears heard him running, and when he had nearly

reached the cabin, they came round the corner of it to see what was the matter. He was up a pine tree in an instant. After a few growls the bears moved off and disappeared behind a vacant cabin. As they had gone behind the cabin which contained the loaded gun, Sullivan thought it would be dangerous to try to make the cabin, for if the door should be swelled fast, the bears would surely get him. Waiting until he thought it safe to return, he dropped to the ground and made a dash for his own cabin. The bears heard him and again gave chase, with the evident intention of getting even for all their annoyances. It was only a short distance to his cabin, but the bears were at his heels when he dived in through the broken window.

A bundle of old newspapers was then set on fire and thrown among the bears, to scare them away. There was some snarling, until one of the young bears with a stroke of a fore paw scattered the blazing papers in all directions; then the bears walked round the cabin-corner out of sight and remained quiet for several minutes.

Just as Jason was saying, " I hope they are

gone for good," there came a thump on the roof which told the prospectors that the bears were still intent on the hams. The bears began to claw the earth off the roof. If they were allowed to continue, they would soon clear off the earth and would then have a chance to tear out the poles. With a few poles torn out, the bears would tumble into the cabin, or perhaps their combined weight might cause the roof to give way and drop them into the cabin. Something had to be done to stop their clawing and if possible get them off the roof. Bundles of hay were taken out of the bed mattress. From time to time Sullivan would set fire to one of these bundles, lean far out through the window, and throw the blazing hay upon the roof among the bears. So long as he kept these fireworks going, the bears did not dig ; but they stayed on the roof and became furiously angry. The supply of hay did not last long, and as soon as the annoyance from the bundles of fire ceased, the bears attacked the roof again with renewed vigor.

Then it was decided to prod the bears with red-hot drills thrust up between the poles of the roof. As there was no firewood in the cabin, and as fuel was necessary in order to heat the drills, a part of the floor was torn up for that purpose.

The young bears soon found hot drills too warm for them and scrambled or fell off the roof. But the old one persisted. In a little while she had clawed off a large patch of earth and was tearing the poles with her teeth.

The hams had been hung up on the wall in the end of the cabin; the old bear was tearing just above them. Jason threw the hams on the floor and wanted to throw them out of the window. He thought that the bears would leave contented if they had them. Sullivan thought differently; he said that it would take six hams apiece to satisfy the bears, and that two hams would be only a taste which would make the bears more reckless than ever. The hams stayed in the cabin.

The old bear had torn some of the poles in two and was madly tearing and biting at others. Sullivan was short and so were the drills. To get within easier reach, he placed the table almost under the gnawing bear, sprang upon it, and called to Jason for a red-hot drill. Jason was about to hand him one when he noticed a small bear climbing in at the window, and, taking the drill with him, he sprang over to beat the bear back. Sullivan jumped down to the fire for a drill, and in climbing back on the table he looked up at the gnawed hole and received a shower of dirt in his face and eyes. This made him flinch and he lost his balance and upset the table. He quickly straightened the table and sprang upon it, drill in hand. The old bear had a paw and arm thrust down through the hole between the poles. With a blind stroke she struck the drill and flung it and Sullivan from the table. He shouted to Jason for help, but Jason, with both young bears trying to get in at the window at once, was striking right and left. He had bears and troubles of his own and did not heed Sullivan's call. The old bear thrust her head down through the hole and seemed about to fall in, when Sullivan in desperation grabbed both hams and threw them out of the window.

The young bears at once set up a row over the hams, and the old bear, hearing the fight, jumped off the roof and soon had a ham in her mouth.

While the bears were fighting and eating, Sullivan and Jason tore up the remainder of the floor and barricaded the window. With both door and window closed, they could give their attention to the roof. All the drills were heated, and both stood ready to make it hot for the bears when they should again climb on the roof. But the bears did not return to the roof. After eating the last morsel of the hams they walked round to the cabin door, scratched it gently, and then became quiet. They had lain down by the door.

It was two o'clock in the morning. The inside of the cabin was in utter confusion. The floor was strewn with wreckage; bedding, drills, broken boards, broken plates, and hay were scattered about. Sullivan gazed at the chaos and remarked that it looked like poor housekeeping. But he was tired, and, asking Jason to keep watch for a while, he lay down on the blankets and was soon asleep.

Toward daylight the bears got up and walked a few times round the cabin. On each round they clawed at the door, as though to tell Sullivan that they were there, ready for his hospitality. They whined a little, half good-naturedly, but no one admitted them, and finally, just before sunrise, they took their departure and went leisurely smelling their way down the trail.

Mountain Parks and Camp-Fires

Mountain Parks and Camp-Fires

THE Rockies of Colorado cross the State from north to south in two ranges that are roughly parallel and from thirty to one hundred miles apart. There are a number of secondary ranges in the State that are just as marked, as high, and as interesting as the main ranges, and that are in every way comparable with them except in area. The bases of most of these ranges are from ten to sixty miles across. The lowlands from which these mountains rise are from five to six thousand feet above sea-level, and the mountain-summits are from eleven thousand to thirteen thousand feet above the tides. In the entire mountain area of the State there are more than fifty peaks that are upward of fourteen thousand feet in height. Some of these mountains are rounded, undulating, or table-topped, but for the most part the higher slopes and culminating summits are

233

broken and angular. Altogether, the Rocky Mountain area in Colorado presents a delightful diversity of parks, peaks, forests, lakes, streams, cañons, slopes, crags, and glades.

On all of the higher summits are records of the ice age. In many places glaciated rocks still retain the polish given them by the Ice King. Such rocks, as well as gigantic moraines in an excellent state of preservation, extend from altitudes of twelve or thirteen thousand feet down to eight thousand, and in places as low as seven thousand feet. Some of the moraines are but enormous embankments a few hundred feet high and a mile or so in length. Many of these are so raw, bold, and bare, they look as if they had been completed or uncovered within the last year. Most of these moraines, however, especially those below timber-line, are well forested. No one knows just how old they are, but, geologically speaking, they are new, and in all probability were made during the last great ice epoch, or since that time. Among the impressive records of the ages that are carried by these mountains, those made by the Ice King probably

stand first in appealing strangely and strongly
to the imagination.

All the Rocky Mountain lakes are glacier lakes.
There are more than a thousand of these. The
basins of the majority of them were excavated
by ice from solid rock. Only a few of them have
more than forty acres of area, and, with the exception of a very small number, they are situated well up on the shoulders of the mountains
and between the altitudes of eleven thousand and
twelve thousand feet. The lower and middle
slopes of the Rockies are without lakes.

The lower third of the mountains, that is, the
foothill section, is only tree-dotted. But the middle portion, that part which lies between the altitudes of eight thousand and eleven thousand
feet, is covered by a heavy forest in which lodge-
pole pine, Engelmann spruce, and Douglas spruce
predominate. Fire has made ruinous inroads into
the primeval forest which grew here.

A large portion of the summit-slopes of the
mountains is made up of almost barren rock, in
old moraines, glaciated slopes, or broken crags,
granite predominating. These rocks are well

tinted with lichen, but they present a barren appearance. In places above the altitude of eleven thousand feet the mountains are covered with a profuse array of alpine vegetation. This is especially true of the wet meadows or soil-covered sections that are continually watered by melting snows.

In the neighborhood of a snowdrift, at an altitude of twelve thousand feet, I one day gathered in a small area one hundred and forty-two varieties of plants. Areas of "eternal snows," though numerous, are small, and with few exceptions, above twelve thousand feet. Here and there above timber-line are many small areas of moorland, which, both in appearance and in vegetation, seem to belong in the tundras of Siberia.

While these mountains carry nearly one hundred varieties of trees and shrubs, the more abundant kinds of trees number less than a score. These are scattered over the mountains between the altitudes of six thousand and twelve thousand feet, while, charming and enlivening the entire mountain-section, are more than a thousand varieties of wild flowers.

Mountain Parks and Camp-Fires

Bird-life is abundant on the Rockies. No State east of the Mississippi can show as great a variety as Colorado. Many species of birds well known in the East are found there, though, generally, they are in some way slightly modified. Most Rocky Mountain birds sound their notes a trifle more loudly than their Eastern relatives. Some of them are a little larger, and many of them have their colors slightly intensified.

Many of the larger animals thrive on the slopes of the Rockies. Deer are frequently seen. Bob-cats, mountain lions, and foxes leave many records. In September bears find the choke-cherry bushes and, standing on their hind legs, feed eagerly on the cherries, leaves, and good-sized sections of the twigs. The ground-hog apparently manages to live well, for he seems always fat. There is that wise little fellow the coyote. He probably knows more than he is given credit for knowing, and I am glad to say for him that I believe he does man more good than harm. He is a great destroyer of meadow mice. He digs out gophers. Sometimes his meal is made upon rabbits or grasshoppers, and I have seen him feeding upon wild plums.

Wild Life on the Rockies

There are hundreds of ruins of the beaver's engineering works. Countless dams and fillings he has made. On the upper St. Vrain he still maintains his picturesque rustic home. Most of the present beaver homes are in high, secluded places, some of them at an altitude of eleven thousand feet. In midsummer, near most beaver homes one finds columbines, fringed blue gentians, orchids, and lupines blooming, while many of the ponds are green and yellow with pond-lilies.

During years of rambling I have visited and enjoyed all the celebrated parks of the Rockies, but one, which shall be nameless, is to me the loveliest of them all. The first view of it never fails to arouse the dullest traveler. From the entrance one looks down upon an irregular depression, several miles in length, a small undulating and beautiful mountain valley, framed in peaks with purple forested sides and bristling snowy grandeur. This valley is delightfully open, and has a picturesque sprinkling of pines over it, together with a few well-placed cliffs and crags. Its swift, clear, and winding brooks are fringed

ESTES PARK AND THE BIG THOMPSON RIVER
FROM THE TOP OF MT. OLYMPUS

with birch and willow. A river crosses it with many a slow and splendid fold of silver.

Not only is the park enchanting from the distance, but every one of its lakes and meadows, forests and wild gardens, has a charm and a grandeur of its own. There are lakes of many kinds. One named for the painter, now dead, who many times sketched and dreamed on its shores, is a beautiful ellipse; and its entire edge carries a purple shadow matting of the crowding forest. Its placid surface reflects peak and snow, cloud and sky, and mingling with these are the green and gold of pond-lily glory. Another lake is stowed away in an utterly wild place. It is in a rent between three granite peaks. Three thousand feet of precipice bristle above it. Its shores are strewn with wreckage from the cliffs and crags above, and this is here and there cemented together with winter's drifted snow. Miniature icebergs float upon its surface. Around it are mossy spaces, beds of sedge, and scattered alpine flowers, which soften a little the fierce aspect of this impressive scene.

On the western margin of the park is a third

lake. This lake and its surroundings are of the highest alpine order. Snow-line and tree-line are just above it. Several broken and snowy peaks look down into it, and splendid spruces spire about its shores. Down to it from the heights and snows above come waters leaping in white glory. It is the centre of a scene of wild grandeur that stirs in one strange depths of elemental feeling and wonderment. Up between the domes of one of the mountains is Gem Lake. It is only a little crystal pool set in ruddy granite with a few evergreens adorning its rocky shore. So far as I know, it is the smallest area of water in the world that bears the name of lake; and it is also one of the rarest gems of the lakelet world.

The tree-distribution is most pleasing, and the groves and forests are a delight. Aged Western yellow pines are sprinkled over the open areas of the park. They have genuine character, marked individuality. Stocky and strong-limbed, their golden-brown bark broken into deep fissures and plateaus, scarred with storm and fire, they make one think and dream more than any other tree on the Rockies. By the brooks the clean and childlike aspens mingle with the willow and the alder or the handsome silver spruce. Some slopes are spread with the green fleece of massed young lodge-pole pines, and here and there are groves of Douglas spruce, far from their better home "where rolls the Oregon." The splendid and spiry Engelmann spruces climb the stern slopes eleven thousand feet above the ocean, where weird timber-line with its dwarfed and distorted trees shows the incessant line of battle between the woods and the weather.

Every season nearly one thousand varieties of beautiful wild flowers come to perfume the air and open their "bannered bosoms to the sun." Many of these are of brightest color. They crowd the streams, wave on the hills, shine in the woodland vistas, and color the snow-edge. Daisies, orchids, tiger lilies, fringed gentians, wild red roses, mariposas, Rocky Mountain columbines, harebells, and forget-me-nots adorn every space and nook.

While only a few birds stay in the park the year round, there are scores of summer visitors who come here to bring up the babies, and to

enliven the air with song. Eagles soar the blue,
and ptarmigan, pipits, and sparrows live on the
alpine moorlands. Thrushes fill the forest aisles
with melody, and by the brooks the ever-joyful
water-ouzel mingles its music with the song of
ever-hurrying, ever-flowing waters. Among the
many common birds are owls, meadowlarks,
robins, wrens, magpies, bluebirds, chickadees,
nuthatches, and several members of the useful
woodpecker family, together with the white-
throated sparrow and the willow thrush.

Speckled and rainbow trout dart in the
streams. Mountain sheep climb and pose on the
crags; bear, deer, and mountain lions are still
occasionally seen prowling the woods or hurrying
across the meadows. The wise coyote is also seen
darting under cover, and is frequently heard
during the night. Here among the evergreens is
found that small and audacious bit of intensely
interesting and animated life, the Douglas squirrel, and also one of the dearest of all small animals, the merry chipmunk. Along the brooks are
a few small beaver colonies, a straggling remnant
of a once numerous population. It is to be hoped

that this picturesque and useful race will be allowed to extend its domain.

The park has also a glacier, a small but genuine chip of the old block, the Ice King. The glacier is well worth visiting, especially late in summer, when the winter mantle is gone from its crevasses, leaving revealed its blue-green ice and its many grottoes. It is every inch a glacier. There are other small glaciers above the Park, but these glacial remnants, though interesting, are not as imposing as the glacial records, the old works which were deposited by the Ice King. The many kinds of moraines here display his former occupation and activities. There are glaciated walls, polished surfaces, eroded basins, and numerous lateral moraines. One of the moraines is probably the largest and certainly one of the most interesting in the Rockies. It occupies about ten square miles on the eastern slope of the mountain. Above timber-line this and other moraines seem surprisingly fresh and new, as though they had been formed only a few years, but below tree-line they are forested, and the accumulation of humus upon them shows that they have long been bearers of trees.

Wild Life on the Rockies

The rugged Peak looks down over all this wild garden, and is a perpetual challenge to those who go up to the sky on mountains. It is a grand old granite peak. There are not many mountains that require more effort from the climber, and few indeed can reward him with such a far-spreading and magnificent view.

One of the most interesting and impressive localities in the Rockies lies around Mt. Wetterhorn, Mt. Coxcomb, and Uncompahgre Peak. Here I have found the birds confiding, and most wild animals so tame that it was a joy to be with them. But this was years ago, and now most of the wild animals are wilder and the birds have found that man will not bear acquaintance. Most of this region was recently embraced in the Uncompahgre National Forest. It has much for the scientist and nature-lover: the mountain-climber will find peaks to conquer and cañons to explore; the geologist will find many valuable stone manuscripts; the forester who interviews the trees will have from their tongues a story worth while; and here, too, are some of Nature's best pictures for those who revel only in the lovely and the wild.

244

IN THE UNCOMPAHGRE MOUNTAINS

Mountain Parks and Camp-Fires

It is a strikingly picturesque by-world, where there are many illuminated and splendid fragments of Nature's story. He who visits this section will first be attracted by an array of rock-formations, and, wander where he will, grotesque and beautiful shapes in stone will frequently attract and interest his attention.

The rock-formation is made up of mixtures of very unequally tempered rock metal, which weathers in strange, weird, and impressive shapes. Much of this statuary is gigantic and uncouth, but some of it is beautiful. There are minarets, monoliths, domes, spires, and shapeless fragments. In places there are, seemingly, restive forms not entirely free from earth. Most of these figures are found upon the crests of the mountains, and many of the mountain-ridges, with their numerous spikes and gigantic monoliths, some of which are tilted perilously from the perpendicular, give one a feeling of awe. Some of the monoliths appear like broken, knotty tree-trunks. Others stand straight and suggest the Egyptian obelisks. They hold rude natural hieroglyphics in relief. One mountain, which is known as Turret-Top, is crowned with what from a distance seems to be a gigantic picket-fence. This fence is formed by a row of monolithic stones.

One of the most remarkable things connected with this strange locality is that its impressive landscapes may be overturned or blotted out, or new scenes may be brought forth, in a day. The mountains do not stand a storm well. A hard rain will dissolve ridges, lay bare new strata, undermine and overturn cliffs. It seems almost a land of enchantment, where old landmarks may disappear in a single storm, or an impressive landscape come forth in a night. Here the god of erosion works incessantly and rapidly, dissecting the earth and the rocks. During a single storm a hilltop may dissolve, a mountain-side be fluted with slides, a grove be overturned and swept away by an avalanche, or a lake be buried forever. This rapid erosion of slopes and summits causes many changes and much upbuilding upon their bases. Gulches are filled, water-courses invaded, rivers bent far to one side, and groves slowly buried alive.

One night, while I was in camp on the slope

of Mt. Coxcomb, a prolonged drought was broken by a very heavy rain. Within an hour after the rain started, a large crag near the top of the peak fell and came crashing and rumbling down the slope. During the next two hours I counted the rumbling crash of forty others. I know not how many small avalanches may have slipped during this time that I did not hear. The next day I went about looking at the new landscapes and the strata laid bare by erosion and landslide, and up near the top of this peak I found a large glaciated lava boulder. A lava boulder that has been shaped by the ice and has for a time found a resting-place in a sedentary formation, then been uplifted to near a mountain-top, has a wonder-story of its own. One day I came across a member of the United States Geological Survey who had lost his way. At my camp-fire that evening I asked him to hug facts and tell me a possible story of the glaciated lava boulder. The following is his account:—

The shaping of that boulder must have antedated by ages the shaping of the Sphinx, and its story, if acceptably told, would seem more like fancy than fact. If the boulder were to relate, briefly, its experiences, it might say: " I helped burn forests and strange cities as I came red-hot from a volcano's throat, and I was scarcely cool when disintegration brought flowers to cover my dead form. By and by a long, long winter came, and toward the close of it I was sheared off, ground, pushed, rolled, and rounded beneath the ice. 'Why are you grinding me up?' I asked the glacier. 'To make food for the trees and the flowers during the earth's next temperate epoch,' it answered. One day a river swept me out of its delta and I rolled to the bottom of the sea. Here I lay for I know not how long, with sand and boulders piling upon me. Here heat, weight, and water fixed me in a stratum of materials that had accumulated below and above me. My stratum was displaced before it was thoroughly solidified, and I felt myself slowly raised until I could look out over the surface of the sea. The waves at once began to wear me, and they jumped up and tore at me until I was lifted above their reach. At last, when I was many thousand feet above the waves, I came to a standstill. Then my mountain-top was much higher than at present. For a long time I looked down upon a tropical world. I am now wondering if the Ice King will come for me again."

The Engelmann spruce forest here is an exceptionally fine one, and the geologist and I discussed it and trees in general. Some of the Indian tribes of the Rockies have traditions of a "Big Fire" about four centuries ago. There is some evidence of a general fire over the Rockies about the time that the Indian's tradition places it, but in this forest there were no indications that there had ever been a fire. Trees were in all stages of growth and decay. Humus was deep. Here I found a stump of a Douglas spruce that was eleven feet high and about nine feet in diameter. It was so decayed that I could not decipher the rings of growth. This tree probably required at least a thousand years to reach maturity, and many years must have elapsed for its wood to come to the present state of decay. Over this stump was spread the limbs of a live tree that was four hundred years of age.

Trees have tongues, and in this forest I inter-

viewed many patriarchs, had stories from saplings, examined the mouldy, musty records of
many a family tree, and dug up some buried history. The geologist wanted in story form a synop-
sis of what the records said and what the trees
told me, so I gave him this account: —

"We climbed in here some time after the retreat
of the last Ice King and found aspen and lodge-
pole pine in possession. These trees fought us
for several generations, but we finally drove them
out. For ages the Engelmann spruce family has
had undisputed possession of this slope. We
stand amid three generations of mouldering ancestors, and beneath these is the sacred mould
of older generations still.

"One spring, when most of the present grown-
up trees were very young, the robins, as they flew
north, were heard talking of strange men who
were exploring the West Indies. A few years later
came the big fire over the Rockies, which for
months choked the sky with smoke. Fire did not
get into our gulch, but from birds and bears which
crowded into it we learned that straggling trees
and a few groves on the Rockies were all that had

A GRASS-PLOT AMONG ENGELMANN SPRUCE

escaped with their lives. Since we had been spared, we all sent out our seed for tree-colonies as rapidly as we could, and in so doing we received much help from the birds, the squirrels, and the bears, so that it was not long before we again had our plumes waving everywhere over the Rockies. About a hundred and sixty years ago, an earthquake shook many of us down and wounded thousands of others with the rock bombardment from the cliffs. The drought a century ago was hard on us, and many perished for water. Not long after the drought we began to see the trappers, but they never did us any harm. Most of them were as careful of our temples as were the Indians. While the trappers still roamed, there came a very snowy winter, and snow-slides mowed us down by thousands. Many of us were long buried beneath the snow. The old trees became dreadfully alarmed, and they feared that the Ice King was returning. For weeks they talked of nothing else, but in the spring, when the mountain-sides began to warm and peel off in earth-avalanches, we had a real danger to discuss.

"Shortly after the snowy winter, the gold-seekers came with their fire havoc. For fifty years we have done our best to hold our ground, but beyond our gulch relentless fire and flashing steel, together with the floods with which outraged Nature seeks to revenge herself, have slain the grand majority, and much, even, of the precious dust of our ancestors has been washed away."

With the exception of the night I had the geologist, my days and nights in this locality were spent entirely alone. The blaze of the camp-fire, moonlight, the music and movement of the winds, light and shade, and the eloquence of silence all impressed me more deeply here than anywhere else I have ever been. Every day there was a delightful play of light and shade, and this was especially effective on the summits; the ever-changing light upon the serrated mountain-crests kept constantly altering their tone and outline. Black and white they stood in midday glare, but a new grandeur was born when these tattered crags appeared above storm-clouds. Fleeting glimpses of the crests through a surging storm arouse strange feelings, and one is at bay, as though

having just awakened amid the vast and vague
on another planet. But when the long, white evening light streams from the west between the
minarets, and the black buttressed crags wear the
alpine glow, one's feelings are too deep for words.

The wind sometimes flowed like a torrent across
the ridges, surging and ripping between the minarets, then bearing down like an avalanche upon
the purple sylvan ocean, where it tossed the trees
with boom, roar, and wild commotion. I usually
camped where it showed the most enthusiasm.
Here I often enjoyed the songs or the fierce
activities of the wind. The absence and the presence of wind ever stirred me strongly. Weird and
strange are the feelings that flow as the winds
sweep and sound through the trees. The Storm
King has a bugle at his lips, and a deep, elemental
hymn is sung while the blast surges wild through
the pines. Mother Nature is quietly singing, singing soft and low while the breezes pause and play
in the pines. From the past one has been ever
coming, with the future destined ever to go when,
with centuries of worshipful silence, one waits for
the winds in the pines. Ever the good old world

grows better both with songs and with silence in the pines.

Here the energy and eloquence of silence was at its best. That all-pervading presence called silence has its happy home within the forest. Silence sounds rhythmic to all, and attunes all minds to the strange message, the rhapsody of the universe. Silence is almost as kind to mortals as its sweet sister sleep.

A primeval spruce forest crowds all the mountain-slopes of the Uncompahgre region from an altitude of eight thousand feet to timber-line. So dense is this forest that only straggling bits of sun-fire ever fall to the ground. Beneath these spiry, crowding trees one has only "the twilight of the forest noon." This forest, when seen from near-by mountain-tops, seems to be a great ragged, purple robe hanging in folds from the snow-fields, while down through it the white streams rush. A few crags pierce it, sun-filled grass-plots dot its expanse at intervals, and here and there it is rent with a vertical avalanche lane.

Many a happy journey and delightful climb I have had in the mountains all alone by moon-

light, and in the Uncompahgre district I had
many a moonlight ramble. I know what it is to be
alone on high peaks with the moon, and I have
felt the spell that holds the lonely wanderer when,
on a still night, he feels the wistful, tender touch
of the summer air, while the leaves whisper and
listen in the moonlight, and the moon-toned etch-
ings of the pines fall upon the magic forest floor.

One of the best moonlit times that I have
had in this region was during my last visit to it.
One October night I camped in a grass-plot in the
depths of a spruce forest. The white moon rose
grandly from behind the minareted mountain,
hesitated for a moment among the tree-spires,
then tranquilly floated up into space. It was a
still night. There was silence in the treetops.
The river near by faintly murmured in repose.
Everything was at rest. The grass-plot was full
of romantic light, and on its eastern margin was
an etching of spiry spruce. A dead and broken
tree on the edge of the grass-plot looked like a
weird prowler just out of the woods, and seemed
half-inclined to come out into the light and speak
to me. All was still. The moonlit mist clung fan-

tastically to the mossy festoons of the fir trees. I was miles from the nearest human soul, and as I stood in the enchanting scene, amid the beautiful mellow light, I seemed to have been wafted back into the legend-weaving age. The silence was softly invaded by zephyrs whispering in the treetops, and a few moonlit clouds that showed shadow centre-boards came lazily drifting along the bases of the minarets, as though they were looking for some place in particular, although in no hurry to find it. Heavier cloud-flotillas followed, and these floated on the forest sea, touching the treetops with the gentleness of a lover's hand. I lay down by my camp-fire to let my fancy frolic, and fairest dreams came on.

It was while camping once on the slope of Mt. Coxcomb that I felt most strongly the spell of the camp-fire. I wish every one could have a night by a camp-fire,—by Mother Nature's old hearthstone. When one sits in the forest within the camp-fire's magic tent of light, amid the silent, sculptured trees, there go thrilling through one's blood all the trials and triumphs of our race. The blazing wood, the ragged and changing flame, the storms and calms, the mingling smoke and blaze, the shadow-figures that dance against the trees, the scenes and figures in the fire, — with these, though all are new and strange, yet you feel at home once more in the woods. A camp-fire in the forest is the most enchanting place on life's highway by which to have a lodging for the night.

Notes

Notes are keyed to page and line numbers. For example, 4:3 means page 4, line 3.

Frontispiece. The photograph shows Longs Peak Inn as Mills rebuilt it after the fire of June 1906. Like the other photographs in this volume, it was taken by Mills himself.

Dedication. John Muir (1838–1914), the Scottish-born explorer, naturalist, and writer who served as Mills's life-long inspiration. As noted in the Introduction, the two men first met in December 1889 during a chance encounter on the beach near San Francisco.

"Colorado Snow Observer"

4:3. Louis George Carpenter (1861–1935), a native of Michigan, joined the faculty of Colorado Agricultural College (now Colorado State University) in 1888 to teach irrigation engineering and to conduct irrigation experiments at the Colorado Agricultural Experiment Station. At CAC Carpenter earned a national reputation by organizing the first systematic instructional and research program in irrigation engineering, a subject of major importance to the water-starved West. Between 1903 and 1905, he served as state engineer of Colorado and it was in this capacity that he engaged the services of Enos Mills as a snow observer. A sketch of Carpenter entitled "Master of Irrigation" is included in the Enos Mills Papers.

7:21. The town of Crested Butte is located in west central Colorado, some twenty-two miles north of Gunnison.

9:7. Lead Mountain (12,537 feet) is located on the Continental Divide to the west of Rocky Mountain National Park. It was apparently named by prospectors during the 1870s.

11:7. Mount Lincoln (14,284 feet), located in central Colorado, twelve miles northeast of Leadville, is the highest peak in the Park Range.

14:20. The seventeen-mile trail from Estes Park over the "bleak heights" of Flattop Mountain to Grand Lake by way of the North Inlet was blazed in 1901 by Fred Sprague (1857–1922), who with his brother Abner Sprague had homesteaded in Moraine Park, and Franklin I. Huntington, a surveyor. Mills made this journey in February 1903.

23:14. As noted in the Introduction (n. 7) Wyoming's Medicine Bow National Forest was extended in 1905 to include the wilderness now embraced by Rocky Mountain National Park. In 1910, the year after this volume appeared, the section of the forest reserve in Colorado was renamed the Colorado National Forest. In 1932 it became the Roosevelt National Forest.

"The Story of a Thousand-Year Pine"

31:10. Mesa Verde is the high tableland in extreme southwestern Colorado whose canyons contain extensive and spectacular ruins of pre-Columbian Indian cliff dwellings. Mesa Verde became a national park in 1906.

32:7. Mancos is located near Mesa Verde, twenty-three miles west of Durango.

46:9. The reports of rich gold strikes in the streams near Denver in 1858 and 1859 (many of them inflated by promoters and speculators) attracted hordes of would-be gold seekers to Colorado. As the Introduction notes, these adventurers included Enos Mills's parents.

"The Beaver and His Works"

58: The photograph facing this page is of Lily Lake (with Estes Cone in the background), located some three miles north of Longs Peak Inn.

60:15. Enos Mills worked as a miner for a number of winters beginning in 1887 at the Anaconda Mine in Butte, Montana, south of Helena.

62:5. The allusion is to the enormously influential *The Earth as Modified by Human Action* by George Perkins Marsh (1801–82), which detailed man's negative impact upon the environment and argued the ethics of land use. First published in 1864, it was thoroughly revised (and given its present title) for a new edition published by Scribner, Armstrong and Company in 1874. Six more American editions appeared between 1877 and 1907. Marsh's book became one of the seminal works of the American conservation movement.

66:1. The former name given the upper portion of the Colorado River, which has its source in the northwestern corner of Rocky Mountain National Park. The name was officially changed in 1921.

67:24. "Abou Ben Adhem (may his tribe increase!)" is the first line of a popular poem written in 1838 by English poet Leigh Hunt (1784–1859).

"The Wilds without Firearms"

76:11. Apparently Lake Odessa (pictured on the opposite page) in Rocky Mountain National Park, which sits at an elevation of 10,020 feet.

78:10. Though once believed to have been an extinct volcano, geologists have now established that Specimen Mountain (12,489 feet) and the adjacent Crater to the southwest are formed of ash and volcanic material that took place elsewhere. Early visitors noted the sheep trails leading over into The Crater and the area still remains (as in Enos Mills's day) a good place to watch and photograph bighorn sheep. Specimen Mountain is located just north of Milner Pass on the Continental Divide.

"A Watcher on the Heights"

83:8. According to tradition, the Cache la Poudre River, which flows northeast out of Poudre Lake to the east of the Continental Divide at Milner Pass, was named in 1836 by a party of French trappers from St. Louis who over the course of one winter safely deposited some of their supplies, including a quantity of black gunpowder, close by its banks.

84:7. Hagues Peak (13,560 feet), located in the Mummy Range northwest of Estes Park, is named for Lieutenant Arnold Hague (1840–1917), a geologist, who, as a member of Clarence King's Geological Survey of the Fortieth Parallel, apparently used the mountain as a triangulation point in 1871.

84:11. Longs Peak (14,256 feet), the highest mountain in Rocky Mountain National Park, was named after Major Stephen H. Long (1784–1864), whose scientific party searching for the sources of the Red River, entered Colorado in late June 1820 and on the morning of June 30 made the first recorded sighting of Colorado's Front Range, including its most prominent feature, which fittingly enough now bears his name. Long and his twenty-two-man party made no attempt to climb the mountain. That honor belongs to Major John Wesley Powell (1834–1902), the Civil War veteran, and William N. Byers (1831–1903), the founding editor of the *Rocky Mountain News,* who together with five others made the first known ascent of Longs Peak on August 23, 1868. Longs Peak is now spelled without an apostrophe.

86:8. Originally there were two Poudre Lakes at Milner Pass on the Continental Divide. At the time Trail Ridge Road was built connecting Estes Park and Grand Lake in the early 1930s, the two lakes were engineered into one. In 1965 the U. S. Board of Geographic Names officially changed the name from plural to singular.

91:9. The town of Loveland, Colorado, lies in the foothills of the Front Range east of Estes Park.

93:14. Mount Richthofen (12,940 feet) is located in the Never Summer Range west of Rocky Mountain National Park. It was named for one of two Baron von Richthofens, both of whom were natives of Silesia in eastern Germany: either Baron Ferdinand von Richthofen (1833–1905) or Baron Walter von Richthofen (d. 1895). Which baron was so honored has been a matter of much conjecture. See Arps and Kingery, *High Country Names: Rocky Mountain National Park,* pp. 154–56.

93:18. The Grand Ditch is actually a series of irrigation ditches on the eastern slope of the Never Summer Mountains built between the late 1880s and 1897, totaling some eleven miles and including twelve headgates. In 1923 the Grand Ditch was extended (by virtue of an act of Congress, for the land was now part of Rocky Mountain National Park) to include Long Draw Reservoir northeast of La Poudre Pass, which was opened in 1930. In 1932 three more miles were added to the Grand Ditch, extending it to Baker Park. The Ditch Camp that Mills referred to was located on Lulu Creek, just above the short-lived mining camp called Lulu City.

93:19. Chambers Lake, which empties into Joe Wright Creek, is located in the Roosevelt National Forest to the north of Cameron Pass, one of the major entrances to North Park.

94:3. Trap Creek and Trap Park lie to the east of Chambers Lake.

"Climbing Long's Peak"

99:11. Enos Mills also told his adventures with Harriet Peters in Chapter XV ("Harriet—Little Mountain Climber") of *The Adventures of a Nature Guide* (Garden City, N.Y.: Doubleday, Page and Co., 1920), pp. 229–39. There Mills identifies the date as September 1905.

100:19. No doubt Alpine Brook, which crosses the Longs Peak trail below tree line.

"Midget, the Return Horse"

116:12. The San Juan Mountains, as Mills notes, are a range located in southwestern Colorado and northern New Mexico. The discovery of gold and silver in the mid-1870s led to the establishment of supply centers like Ouray and Silverton and mining camps like Telluride. Ouray and Silverton are located on present Highway 550; Telluride lies a few miles to the west. At the peak of its gold production, about 1890, the population of Telluride exceeded five thousand.

119:5. Alma, located in Park County east of Leadville, was established in 1872 and prospered with the mining activity on nearby Mount Bross.

119:13. The allusion to the Twelve Mile Range is unclear, but the description suggests that Mills is riding up the Park Range toward Hoosier Pass.

119:15. The Hoosier Pass (11,514 feet), like nearby Mount Lincoln (14,286 feet) and Mount Silverheels (13,825 feet), referred to below, are located in the Park Range.

125:2. Leadville in Park County, where silver was discovered in 1875, became one of the most glamorous, profitable, and wide-open mining camps in Colorado. It flourished until the price of silver collapsed in 1893.

125:5. Pike National Forest, located to the northwest of Pikes Peak and Colorado Springs, is named, like the mountain, for Lieutenant Zebulon M. Pike (1779–1813), the first official American explorer to enter Colorado, who sighted Pikes Peak on November 15, 1806, and made an unsuccessful attempt to scale it.

"Faithful Scotch"

131:1. Enos Mills received Scotch as a puppy in 1902, and the dog soon became his constant companion and a fixture at the Inn. Mills taught Scotch to extinguish fires, and his death in 1910 occurred because the dog tried to extinguish the fuse on a charge of dynamite being used by a local road crew.

138:8. The "young lady from Michigan" was Victoria Broughm, or Brougham, who had been staying at Longs Peak Inn. Three of the four guides whom Enos Mills dispatched in search of Miss Broughm (see below) were his younger brother Enoch ("Joe") Mills (1880–1935), William S. Cooper (1884–1978), who pioneered in the exploration of Wild Basin, south of Longs Peak Inn, and went on to become a leading ecologist at the University of Minnesota, and Carl Piltz (186?–1926), who later became Estes Park's leading mason. Mills expanded this chapter, in which he retold the Victoria Broughm rescue story, into a magazine article, "The Story of Scotch," which he published in the May 1, 1912, issue of *Country Life in America* and then into book form, *The Story of Scotch* (Boston: Houghton Mifflin, 1916). Joe Mills includes his own version of the event in his *A Mountain Boyhood* (1926).

145:14. The allusion is to the homestead cabin that Enos Mills built in Longs Peak Valley in 1885–86.

"Bob and Some Other Birds"

154:21. The North Branch of the St. Vrain River originates in the Wild

Basin region of Rocky Mountain National Park, to the south of Longs Peak, and gradually makes its way to the South Platte.

"Kinnikinick"

178:19. The Blackfoot Indians were the largest and most powerful of the tribes inhabiting the northern plains. The Piute (or Paiute) Indians, mentioned below, were a small tribe inhabiting the Great Basin east of the Sierra Nevada, encompassing parts of California, northwestern Nevada, and eastern Oregon. The Alaska Indians, also mentioned below, were members of one of several small tribes inhabiting what was then a U.S. Territory.

"The Lodge-Pole Pine"

184: 23. The quotation is from John Muir's *Our National Parks* (Boston: Houghton Mifflin, 1901), p. 69. The chapter in which it occurs, "The Yellowstone National Park," had originally appeared in *Atlantic Monthly,* 81 (April 1898): 509–22.

"Rocky Mountain Forests"

209:8. This, of course, was the motto of gold seekers crossing the great plains to the gold fields of Colorodo beginning in 1859.

"Besieged by Bears"

217:19. Geneva Park is located southwest of Geneva Mountain in northern Park County. Mills visited the area in the winter of 1902–3 during a six-day, 120-mile inspection trip of the headwaters of the Platte River.
218: Photograph of Ouray, Colorado. See 116:12.

"Mountain Parks and Camp-Fires"

239:8. Bierstadt Lake, located on top of a moraine above Bear Lake in Rocky Mountain National Park, was named after the German-born artist Albert Bierstadt (1830–1902), who had come to Estes Park in the autumn of 1876 to paint a large landscape for the Earl of Dunraven. The major legacy of Bierstadt's visit is the magnificent five-by-eight-foot painting, *Rocky Mountains, Longs Peak,* which now hangs in the Western Room of the Denver Public Library.
239:15. Chasm Lake, which lies in a glacial cirque beneath the East Face of Longs Peak at an elevation of 11,760 feet. Longs Peak (14,256 feet) is

flanked by Mount Lady Washington (13,281 feet) and Mount Meeker (13,911 feet).

240:10. Gem Lake (8,830 feet) is located on Lumpy Ridge just north of the town of Estes Park. It is reputed to be a lake without inlet or outlet.

243:3. There are five living or "true" glaciers within the boundaries of what is now Rocky Mountain National Park: Andrews Glacier, Rowe Glacier, Sprague Glacier, Taylor Glacier, and Tyndall Glacier.

244:9–10. Mount Wetterhorn (14,020 feet), Mount Coxcomb (13,663 feet), and Uncompahgre Peak (14,306) are all located in the San Juan Mountains in southwestern Colorado.

244:17. The Uncompahgre National Forest spans a number of counties in the southwestern corner of Colorado.

245:24. Presumably Turret Peak (13,826 feet), located in La Plata County in southwestern Colorado.

Index

Index

269

Index

Horses, return, 115–118; Midget, 119–128.

Hotel, ejected from a, 11.

Ice, fine arts of, 12.

Kinnikinick, a plant pioneer, 171–175; its nursery for trees, 175, 176; growth of, 176, 177; flowers and fruit of, 177; as a bed, 177, 178; a legend of, 178, 179; reclaiming work of, 180.

Lakes, 235, 239, 240.
Lead Mountain, 9.
Leadville, 125.
Lion, mountain, 6, 20, 23; an epicure, 9, 10; tracked by a, 10.
Long's Peak, 15, 84; a climb up, with a little girl, 99–111; summit of, 109, 110; Scotch and the young lady on, 138–141; a winter climb with Scotch, 142–147; birds on summit of, 158.
Loveland, 91.

Mammals, 237.
Medicine Bow National Forest, 23.
Medicine-men, 10, 11.
Mesa Verde, 31, 48, 49.
Moonlight, the mountains by, 254–256.
Mt. Coxcomb, 244; camping on the slope of, 246–254, 256.
Mt. Lincoln, 11, 123.
Mt. Richthofen, 93.
Mt. Silverheels, 120, 121.
Mt. Wetterhorn, 244.

Ouzel, water, 100–102, 152, 153, 158, 159.

Park, a Rocky Mountain, 238–244.
Pine, nursed by kinnikinick, 175, 176.
Pine, lodge-pole, its names, 183; de-
scription of, 183; its habit of growth, 183, 184; its aggressive character, 184; distribution of, 184, 185, 208; its method of dispersing its seeds, 185–187, 191; growth of, 187, 188, 193, 194; as a colonist and pioneer, 189; cones embedded in, 189, 190; sunlight necessary to, 190; fire in a forest of, 191, 192; enemies of, 193; uses of, 193; value of, 193–195.
Pine, Western yellow, a thousand-year-old, 31–50; habits of the, 200–204; character of the, 240.
Pinus flexilis, 188, 208.
Plants, of the summit-slopes, 235, 236.
Potentilla, 208.
Poudre Lakes, 86.
Poudre Valley, flood in, 83, 95.
Ptarmigan, 9, 107, 153, 158.

Quail, a pet, 161–167.

Rabbit, snowshoe, 9.
Rex, a St. Bernard dog, 160, 164–167.
Rock, easily eroded, 246.
Rock-formations, grotesque and beautiful, 245, 246.
Rocky Mountains, individuality of, 213; character of, 233, 234.

Schoolhouse, a mountain, 13.
Sheep, mountain, 9; a flock of, 78.
Silence, 254.
Snow, tracks in, 9.
Snow-cornice, breaking through a, 17.
Snow-fall, 7.
Snow-slides, 19, 20; an adventure with a snow-slide, 24, 25.
Snowstorm, a, 8.
Solitaire, 153–155.
Specimen Mountain, electrical phenomena on, 88–92.

270

Index